Junk Jeans

Junk-Jeans™

Eazy Quilts
&
Wall Hangings

Designs & Instructions
By

Luveta Nickels

Introduction

For the most part I consider myself a garment sewer. I'm a beginner at quilting and my objective was to design some projects to inspire those hesitating to get started. The finishes to the following projects are Fun and Foolproof and now that I've gained some confidence in the quilting avenue I join others in my excitement to cut, create and recycle in different ways. My hope is to inspire you to use these ideas in your own flamboyant way to express yourself. Cut or tear jeans, add some fabric and watch your projects evolve. There aren't any fabric police to judge your combinations or teachers waiting to grade your work so run to your favorite store or explore the stash I know you have and design your own Recycling Reward.

Credits and Grateful Thanks

Tina Petrello............. Graphic Designer
Natalie Sorenson................. Illustrator
Tracy Nickels........................ Editing
Danna Nickels........................ Editing
Donna Nickels........................ Editing
Steve Wicks (Hubby)................Photos

I would like to thank all the sewing machine companies that continue to support me and product companies that supply materials for ongoing projects. Friends and family that encourage me to keep focused when I'm in the crazed phase of an outrageous idea. I want to thank our good neighbors the Webers for coming to the rescue during camera crisis. And, most of all, thanks to my loyal customers, students and fellow seamstress friends who continue to purchase my products. You allow me the privilege of sharing my passion. If you have any questions or suggestions, I would love to hear from you. Please call 605-532-5625 or email luveta@itctel.com. Visit us online at www.junkjeanspeople.com.

Luveta Nickels

The Junk Jeans People, GET N' EVEN Publishing

RR #3 Box 105
Clark, SD 57225
ISBN: 1-928727-03-4
Printed in Sioux Falls, SD USA

Dedication

This book is dedicated to the loving memory of my best friend Deb Reidburn. I'm grateful to have had the privilege of her friendship. Deb lost her battle with breast cancer on Christmas Eve 1999. Her wish was not for sympathy, but rather for finding a cure for future generations. A portion of this book will be donated to the continued research in finding a cure for this dreadful disease. The Denim Angels thank you for your support and contribution to sewing for the cure!

Let's Get Started

All seam allowances are included and should be sewn using 1/4".

A few ideas to make your projects easier!

I delight in hunting for just the right pair of old jeans. This means color, age, special pockets or sentimental value. You could hunt at yard sales, the Salvation Army, your good neighbor or maybe you already have that special pair in your own collection. Whatever method you chose for finding your perfect pair of old jeans is the fun part! Deciding, designing and creating "Something from Nothing" will be very rewarding. You deserve a Bravo award for helping recycle our environment.

Tools you will find helpful!

Utility knife or point cutter—seam rippers are too weak
Pliers—to help with broken zippers, belt loops and squeezing thick flat felled seams
Quilting Pins—longer heavier pins stand up to heavy denim pieces better
Sharp Scissors—necessary because even old junk-jeans welt seams are tough to cut
Rotary cutter, mat, & rulers—easiest way to measure & cut strips and blocks
Jean-a-ma-jig—helps your machine get over thick jean seams

Prepare:

Get the jeans ready by washing them first. Some projects call for washing the jean sections after they are cut to achieve a fringed unfinished edge.

Cut the legs apart for the appropriate layout according to the project. Lay the jeans flat and press with hot steam and spray starch. I like to use the Miracle Ironing Board Cover. It is a cover made from Fiberglass that won't burn and reflects the heat. The super cushion allows the iron to glide over zippers and rivets.

Cutting Diagrams:

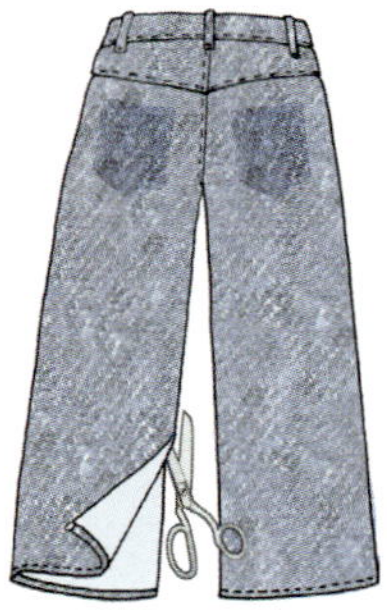

Cutting Option 1

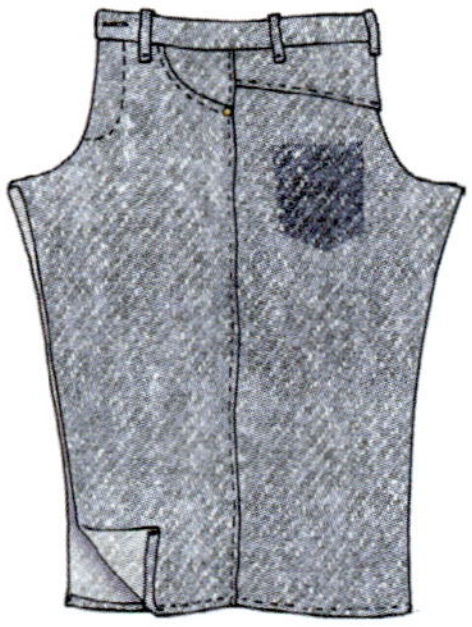

Result of Cutting Option 1

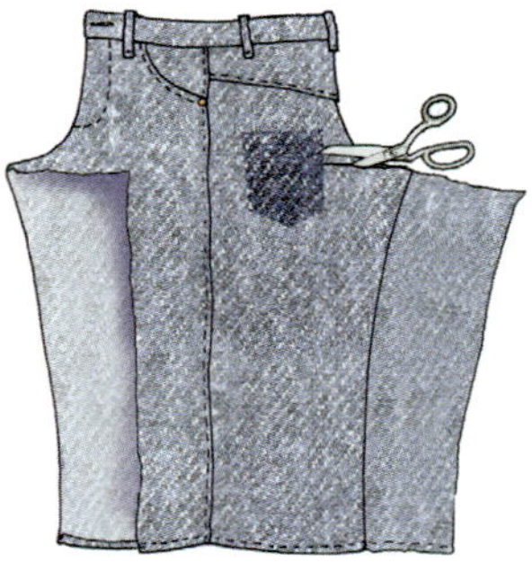

Cutting Option 2

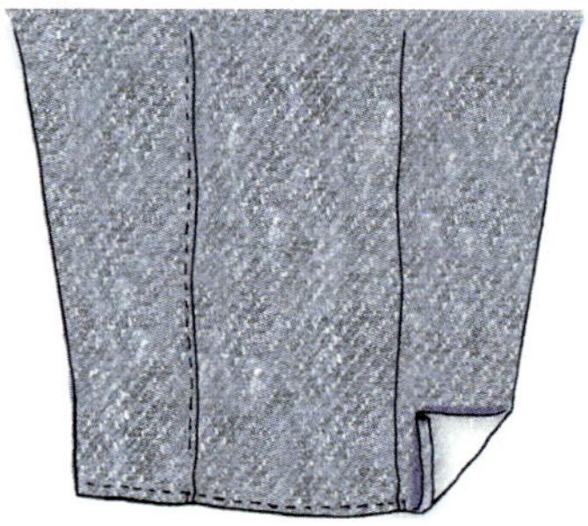

Result of Cutting Option 2

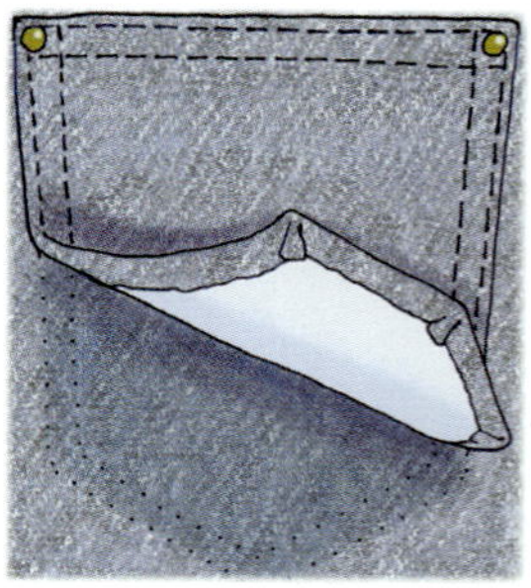

Pocket removal

TABLE OF CONTENTS

Nine Patch Quilt

Nine Patch Quilt

This easy to do Nine Patch Quilt was purchased at a benefit auction for my best friend Deb Reidburn. It was sewn and tied with loving care by her parents, Lyman and Nadine Wookey. The beauty of this simple design comes to life with different shades of blue and it's always a surprise when the blocks create the diagonal repeat. White denim and a purchased sheet were used to enhance the possibilities of this well known design. While this quilt holds many memories, I encourage you to experiment with different colors to make your quilt as special as this one.

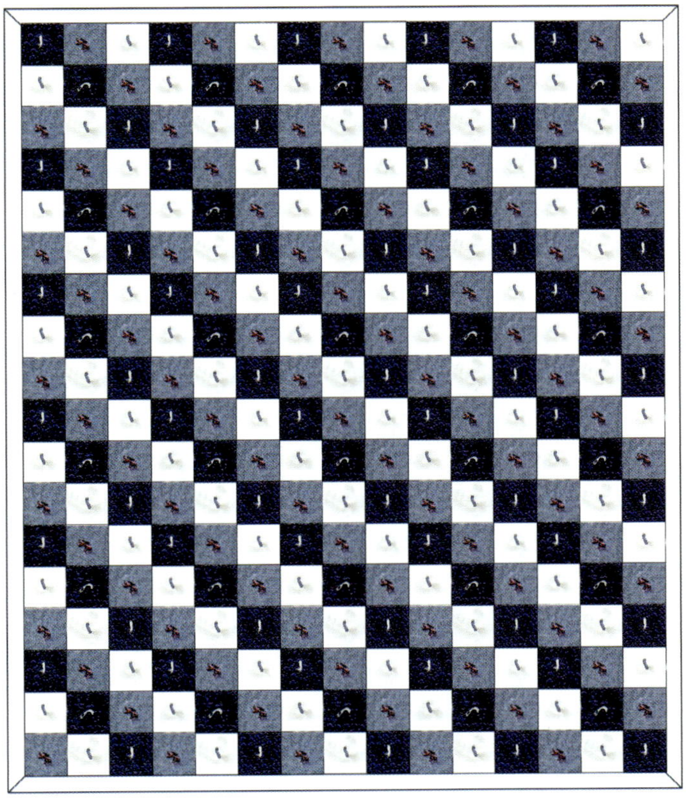

Different sizes can be achieved by adding or deleting complete rows or by adding a border. Try adding another vertical and horizontal row for king-size quilt or subtract two vertical and one horizontal for a twin-size quilt. Borders can be added to achieve more specific sizes.

Materials:

- 6 pairs of dark blue adult jeans
- 6 pairs of light blue adult jeans
- 6 pairs of white adult jeans or 2¼ yard white denim
- 1 queen-size quilt batting 90" x 108"
- 1 king-size sheet or 6 yard of 45" fabric for backing
- 3 colors of yarn or floss for tying
- Latex glove or rubber balloon

Approximate Finished Size 82" x 99"

Nine Patch Quilt continued

Cut:

1. Cut 90 - 6" squares from each color of blue jeans. Refer to diagram. Depending on the condition of your jeans you should be able to get 15 - 6" blocks from each pair. Example: 15 x 6 = 90 and 90 x 3 colors = 270 total. Yea the math worked!

Sew:

2. Assemble 30 blocks in color scheme shown. (Using three white, three light blue and three dark blue). Sew blocks flip flopping the seams and pressing accordingly.

3. Sew vertical rows, then horizontal rows. Refer to diagram.

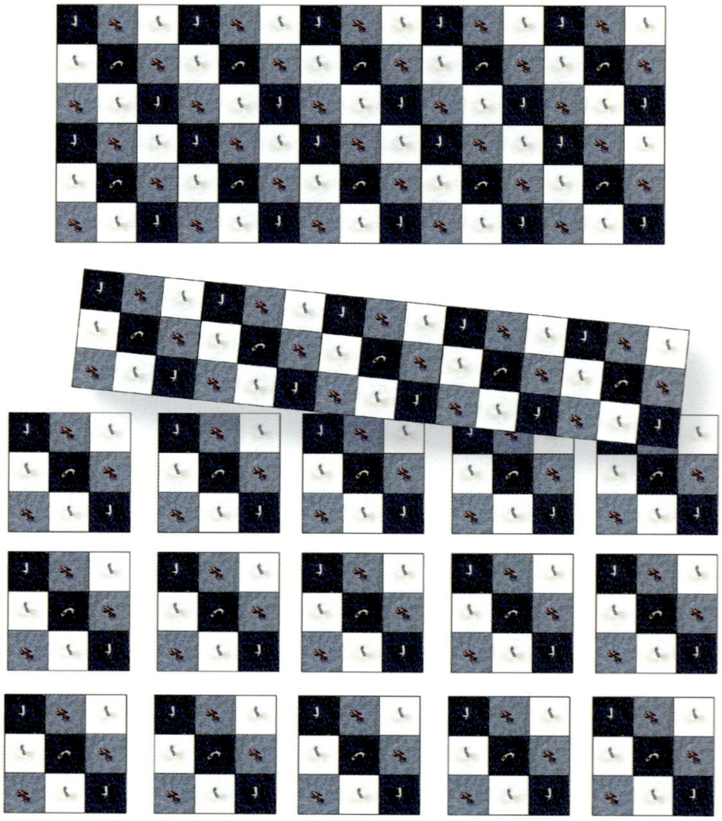

4. Prepare purchased sheet by removing hems on top and bottom and pressing flat.

5. If using yardage for backing, sew two 3 yard sections right sides together down the middle or you can split one 3 yard section lengthwise and piece to either side of the other 3 yard piece. Your backing should measure approximately 90" x 108".

6. Lay backing piece flat on the floor wrong side up and put quilt batting on top.

7. Position quilt blocks in the center.

8. Backing should extend 2" all around quilt. Press under ¼" to wrong side on backing edge.

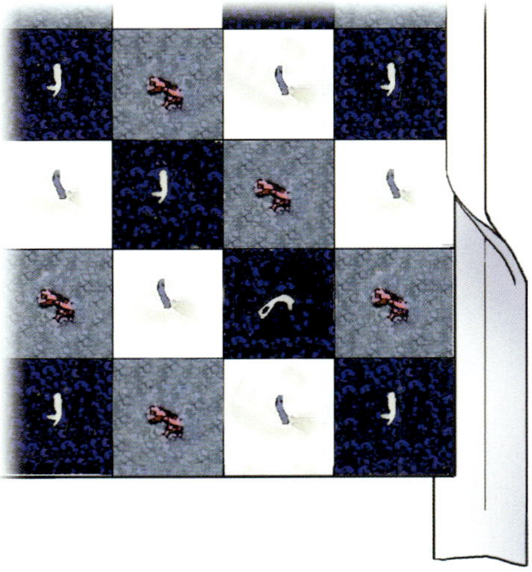

9. Fold 1" on backing and then again around quilt, folding miter at corners.

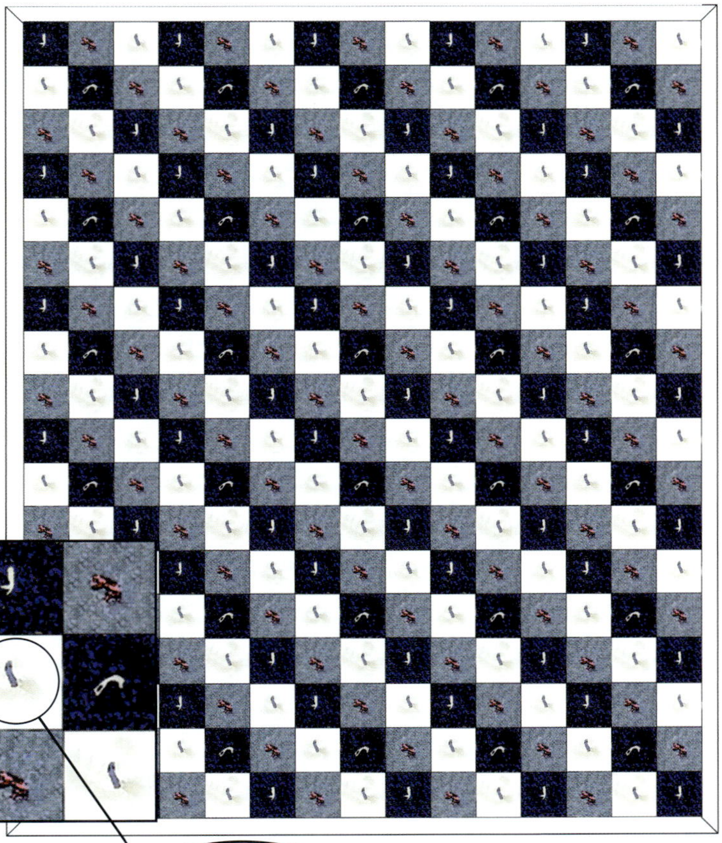

10. Pin securely in place. Topstitch through all layers to form self- binding.

11. Tie in the center of each block using contrasting yarn or floss. Pull tie through all layers of quilt by gripping needle with latex glove or rubber balloon. Use pliers to pull needle through layers if needed.

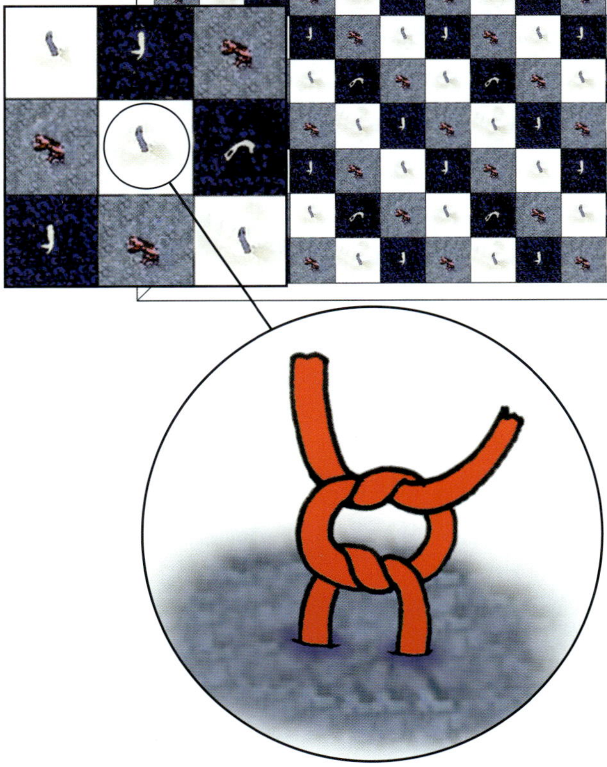

What a nice cozy quilt!

Little Britches Crib Quilt

Little Britches Crib Quilt

This is one of my favorite quilts because of the simplicity of construction. I'm confident most of you will have success even if this is your first try. All decorations are applied after the quilt is completed so there is little room for error. The anticipation of foolproof finishing is easy enough for the beginner and yet a refreshing change for the accomplished Quilter.

Materials

1 pair of junk jeans (I used size 6 slim)
6 pockets
1 package red baby rick rack
4 star buttons, size $1^3/_4$"
1 yard of rope cording for waistline
$^5/_8$ yard red & white check for top and bottom borders
1 yard red corduroy
$^1/_4$ yard blue bandanna
$^1/_4$ yard red & white stripe
$2^1/_4$ yard navy stars for blocks and backing
$^1/_4$ yard red star print
$^1/_4$ yard red bandanna
$^1/_4$ yard blue & white stripe
1 crib-size quilt batting (45"x60")
Approximate Finished Size 44" x 58"

Prepare:

1. Tear or rip inner leg seam on both legs. Rip back crotch and cut through center back waistband. Continue to rip front crotch to bottom of zipper. Breaking the zipper will be required. If jeans do not rip easily use a utility knife to assist you with the stubborn seams. Please use caution. Only half of the jeans will be used in this project.

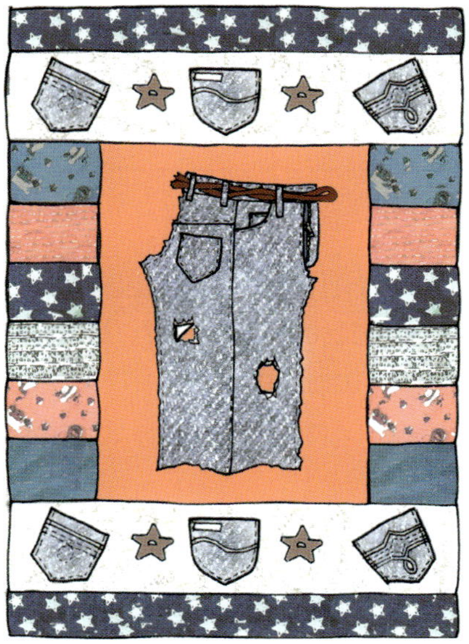

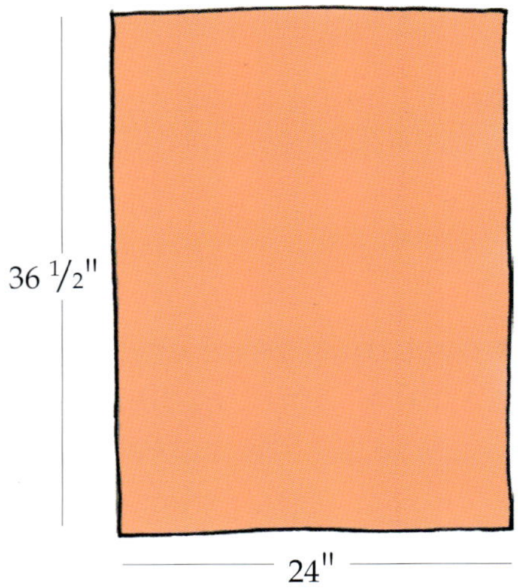

2. Wash this piece to make the edges fray. Press using steam and spray starch.

Cut:

3. Cut red corduroy 24" x 36 1/2"
Cut two blocks of each print 6 1/2" x 11 1/2"
Cut two red checked borders 9 1/2" x 45"

Little Britches Crib Quilt continued

8. Layer backing, and quilt top, right sides together pinning through the batting on sides of quilt only. Fold top and bottom at side edges as shown in diagram.

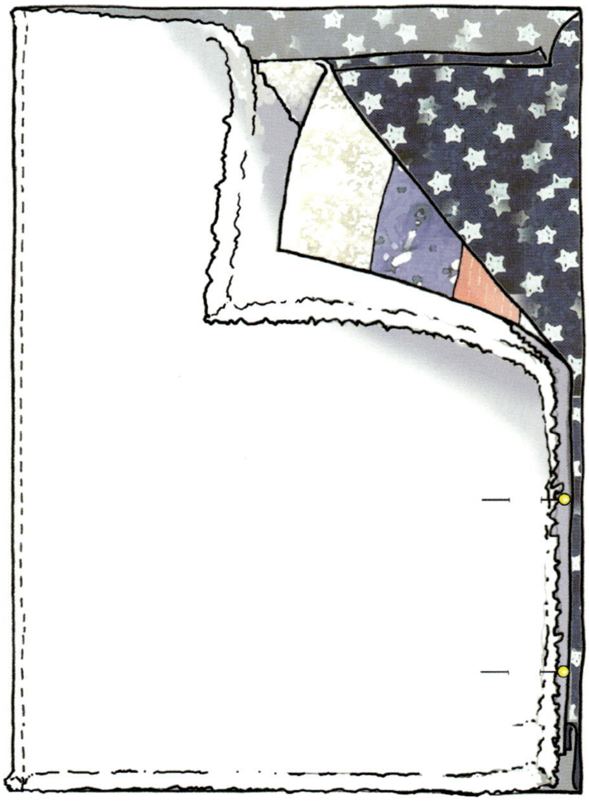

Sew:

4. Stitch or serge 6 ½" blocks together as shown for each side.

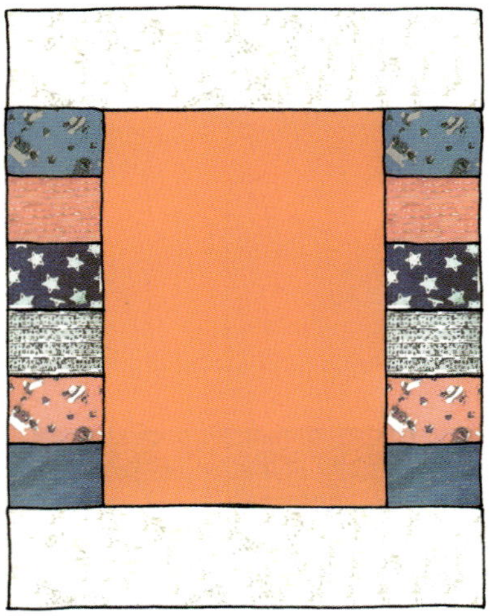

5. Sew the blocks to the long edges of the red corduroy.

6. Stitch red checked border to top and bottom of quilt. Trim excess border after stitching.

7. Lay batting on top of quilt leaving a 3" border of batting extending at the top and bottom of quilt top. Press under ¼" to wrong side of backing fabric across top and bottom.

9. Stitch or serge along both sides of quilt. I like to use my walking foot to keep the layers even.

10. Turn quilt inside out using opening at the top and bottom. At this stage the quilt looks like a giant tube.

11. Fold top border over quilt front encasing the 3" extended batting and topstitch through all layers. Repeat for the bottom border.

12. Stitch in the ditch around red corduroy and between each side block.

13. Zigzag rick rack through the middle of 2 pockets. They will be sewn to the quilt in the center of the top and bottom.

14. Pin pockets and jean leg section in place. Stitch pockets and jean leg section through all layers of the quilt. Topstitch an additional seam along the flat felled side seam of the jean section through all layers. Stitch around the 3 cornered tear holes if the jeans have them.

16. Finish the quilt by adding the rope at waistline.

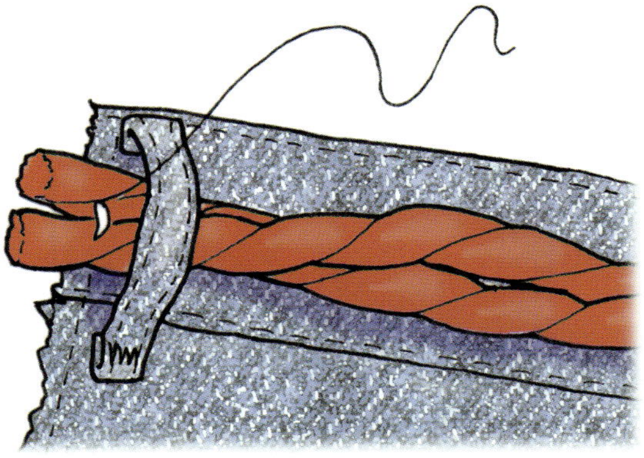

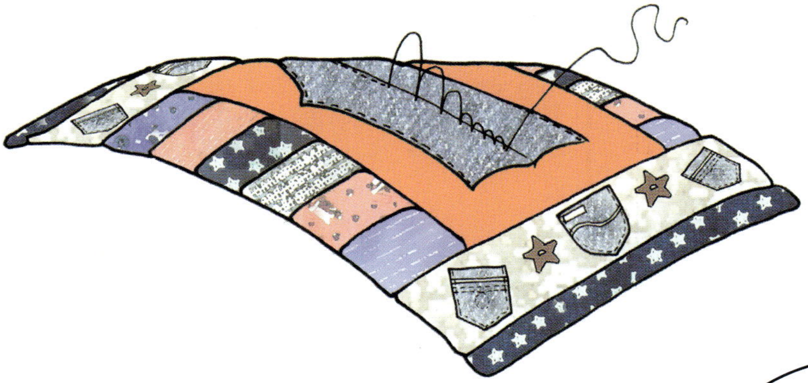

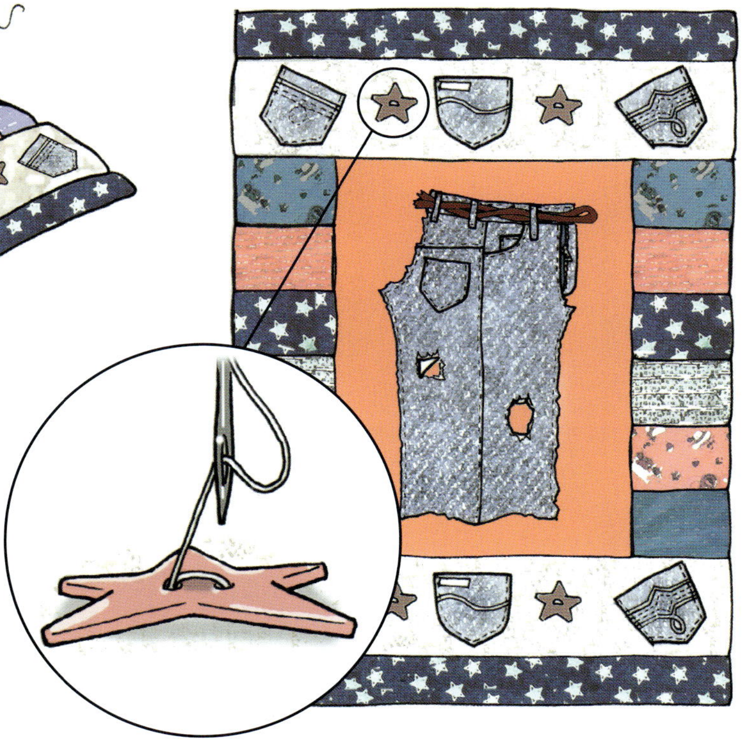

15. Tape the 4 Star buttons in place. Bar tack buttons through all layers with your sewing machine or stitch in place by hand. Remove tape after stitching is done.

With this method you are quilting as you decorate with the surface pieces. Enjoy your Little Britches Quilt!

Topsy Turvy with Reversible Pillow

Reverse side of pillow

Why not take your toddler's first pair of blue jeans and preserve them in an artistic keepsake? The tumbling feel of the leg sections could remind you of how active toddlers are. The mitered corners are especially easy. When cut away from the wall hanging, the corners form the sections of this reversible pillow. This wall hanging has a picture frame procedure and nothing goes to waste!

Topsy Turvy with Reversible Pillow

Materials

1 size 3 or smaller child's jeans
1 yard lime green
1½ yard print for back
(extra required to cut out motifs)
1 yard batting (at least 45" wide)
3/8 yard royal blue for inside border
5 conchos
¼ yard fusible web
¼ yard fusible interfacing
Approximate Finished Size: 38" x 32".

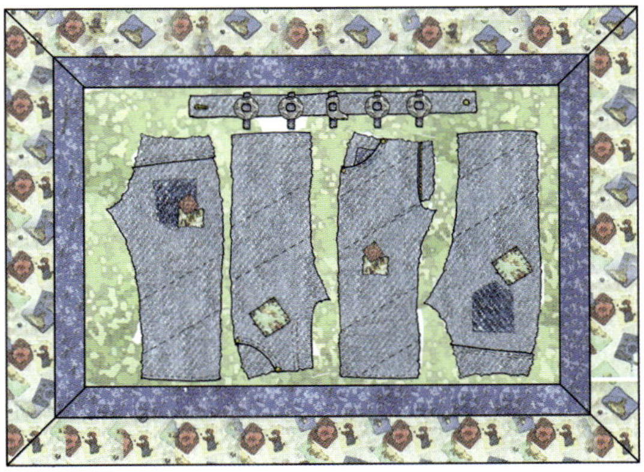

4. Fuse motifs randomly to the four jean sections. Zigzag or use a decorative stitch to appliqué the motifs to the individual jean pieces. I love to decorate while handling one piece at a time.

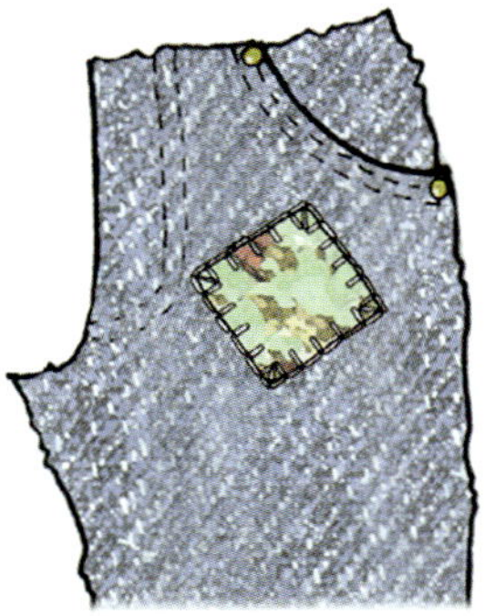

Prepare:

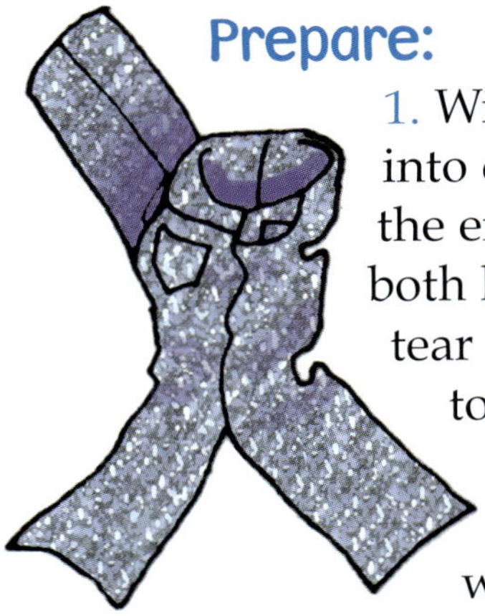

1. With caution tear or rip jeans into quarters. Start by ripping the entire inside leg seam on both legs. Then carefully rip or tear side seams. Rip back crotch to waistband. Rip front crotch to bottom of zipper. Break zipper and unzip to waistband. Remove waistband.

2. Press jean sections with spray starch.

3. Rough cut motif designs to use for appliqués. Press fusible interfacing to wrong side. Press fusible web to wrong side of interfaced designs. Cut around carefully and remove paper backing.

5. Press under sides of legs on all four sections. Press one back crotch to right side leaving raw edge exposed. The raw edge will also be natural at bottom of zipper on front crotch.

6. Leave raw edge at waistline of the four jean sections.

7. Lay these jean sections aside for final step.

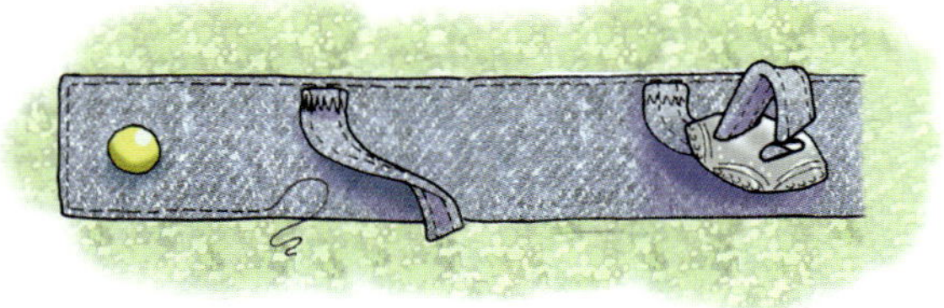

8. Thread conchos onto belt loops. Press waistline seam of waistband together and lay aside.

Topsy Turvy continued

Cut:

9. Cut print backing 42½" x 36½".

10. Cut 4 royal blue strips 2" wide.

11. Cut lime green 25" x 32".

Sew:

12. Stitch royal blue borders to all four edges of backing fabric. Press seams toward royal blue.

13. Press ¼" to wrong side on all royal blue raw edges.

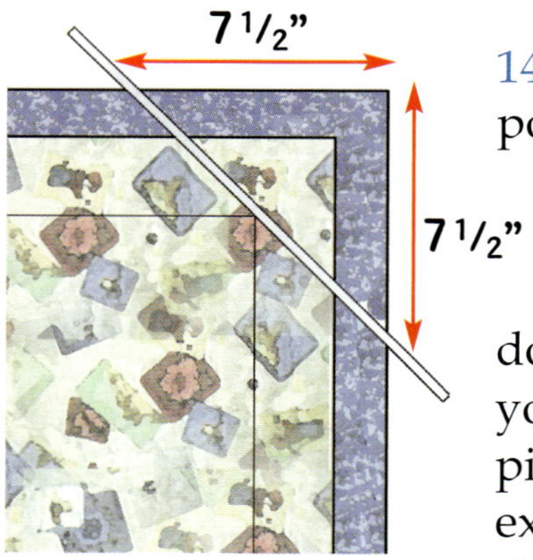

14. Measure from the point of one corner down 7½" and from the same point on the opposite edge down 7½". Connect your marks with a piece of tape letting it extend from the **wrong** side, refer to diagram.

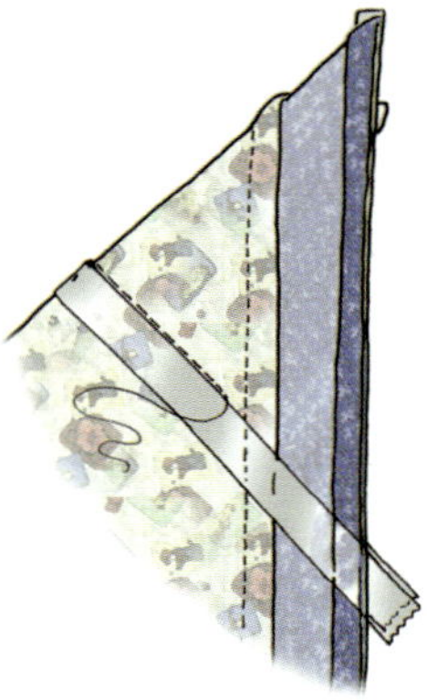

15. Tape right sides of corner together making tape match and stitch along taped edge. Now be brave and carefully cut off the corner. You will be cutting through the backing fabric and

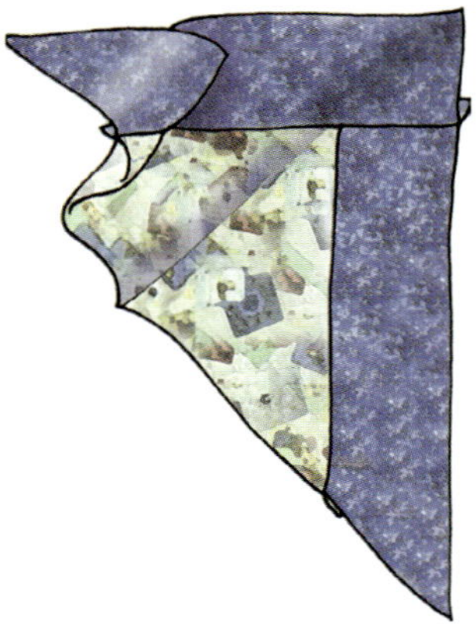

the royal blue inside border. Bravo!! You've just created a perfect miter!

16. Repeat this step for all four corners. Save the corners that you cut off and use them for the reversible pillow.

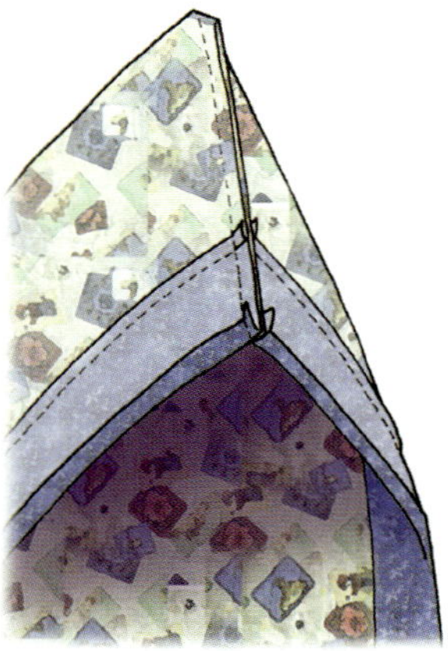

17. Turn and gently press seams in the mitered corners. It should look like a giant "Fabric Frame" with the wrong side facing you in the middle of the frame.

18. Cut batting the same size as "Fabric Frame" and tuck inside making sure it goes all the way into the corners.

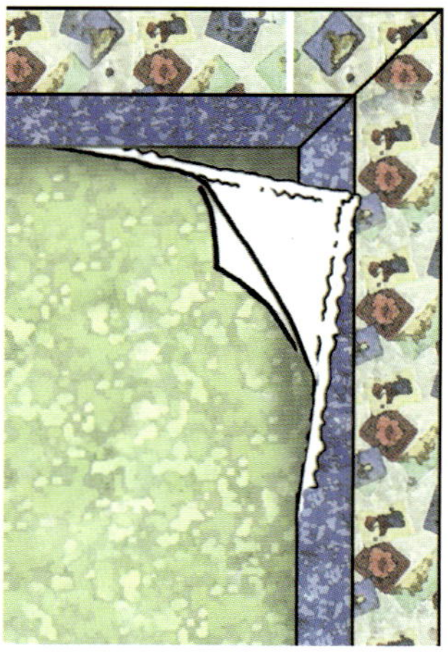

19. Center the lime green fabric on top of the batting and tuck green under the royal blue border. Pin securely in place. Topstitch through all layers gently holding the fabric behind and in front of your foot.
(I like to use the walking foot for pucker free stitching).

20. Stitch in the ditch (between royal blue and print backing) all the way around.

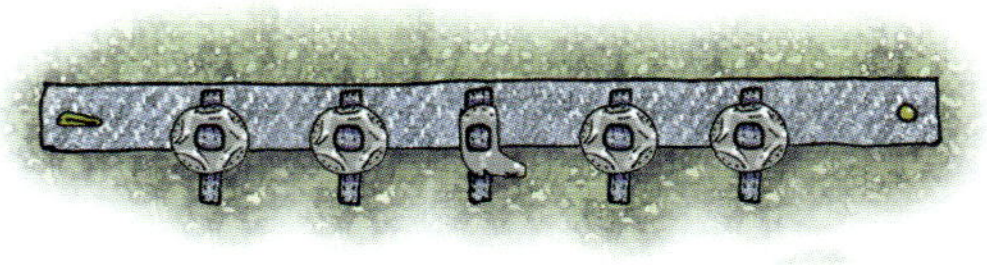

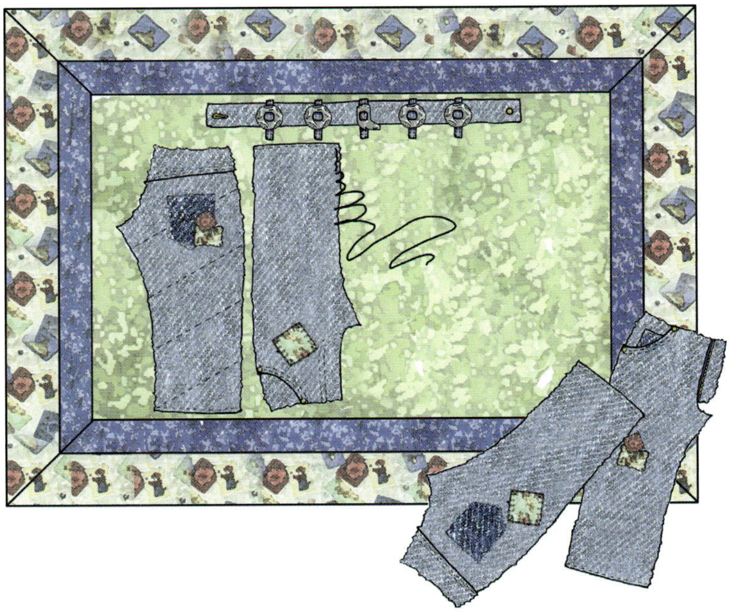

21. Pin waistband close to top edge of wall hanging. Stitch both long edges of waistband, through all layers, being careful not to hit the conchos. Using a Jean-ma-jig to level your sewing machine foot makes stitching through the belt loops a little easier.

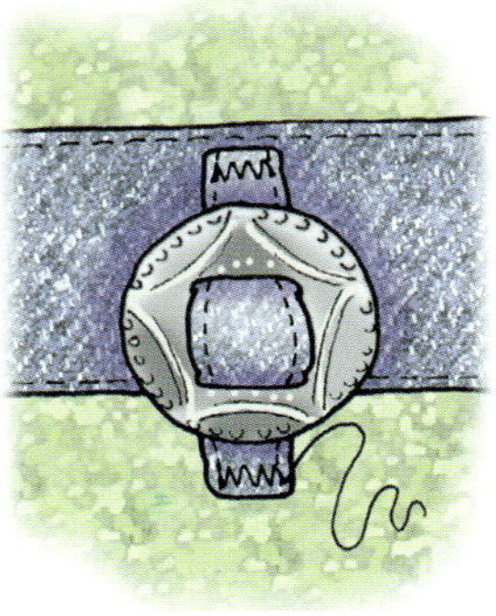

22. Place jean sections on top of lime green as shown. Pin securely and topstitch through all layers. If you get too close to a rivet or can't turn under a raw edge, simply leave it and go on. That's the beauty of old jeans; they are full of character and add to the uniqueness of your project.

23. Stitch diagonal lines randomly through the jean legs between the appliquéd motifs to finish quilting your toddler's keepsake jeans. Congratulations! Now try the matching reversible pillow using some of the leftovers from the wall hanging.

Reversible Pillow

Materials

1 pair adult Junk Jeans
½ yard yellow
1 package double fold bias tape or tubular bias
1 large shank button

Left over corners from Topsy -Turvy Wall Hanging
Pillow form 14" square or bag fiberfill
Finished size: 14" square

Cut:

1. Cut jean leg up center back and lay flat.

2. Cut 14½" square positioning the square so the inside leg seam and the outside leg seam are equal. See diagram.

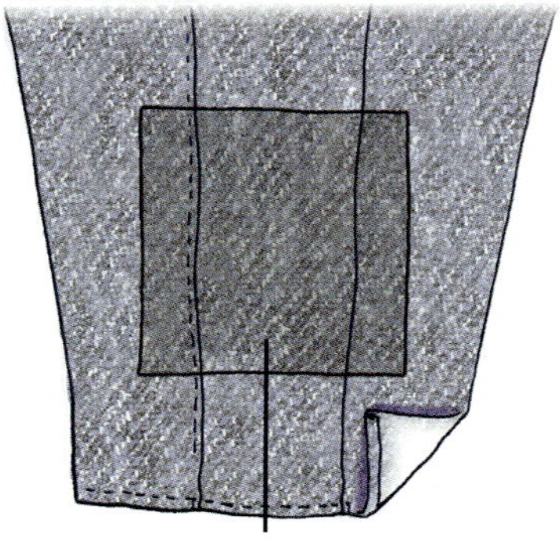

3. Tear off back pockets. (Use a utility knife to loosen bar tacks or cut a hole behind pocket rivets). Rivets will stay in the pockets for decoration.

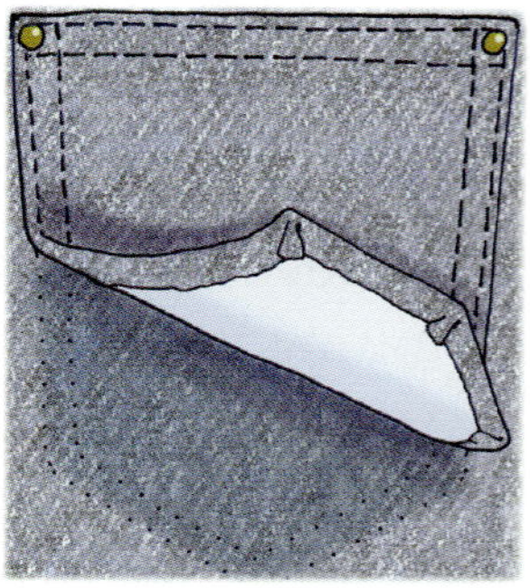

4. Cut a 14½" square from yellow fabric.

Sew:

5. Working on the $14\frac{1}{2}$" jeans square, topstitch double fold or tubular bias along both side seams. One seam will be flat felled and the other seam will be plain.

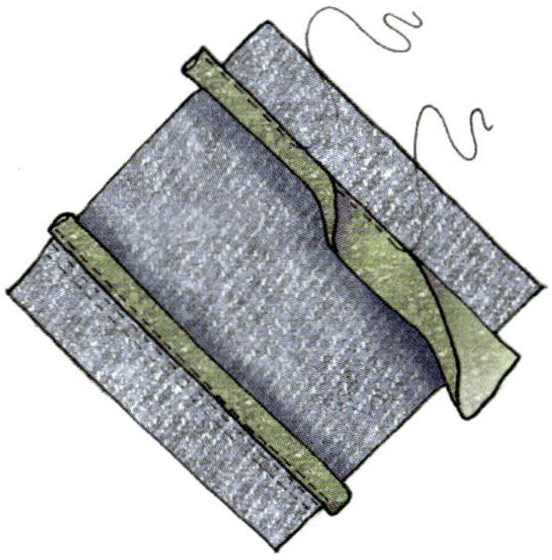

6. **Option:** You can also cut your own strips $1\frac{1}{2}$" wide and press wrong sides together. Place raw edges next to jean seams and stitch. Press folded edge next to jean seams and topstitch in place.

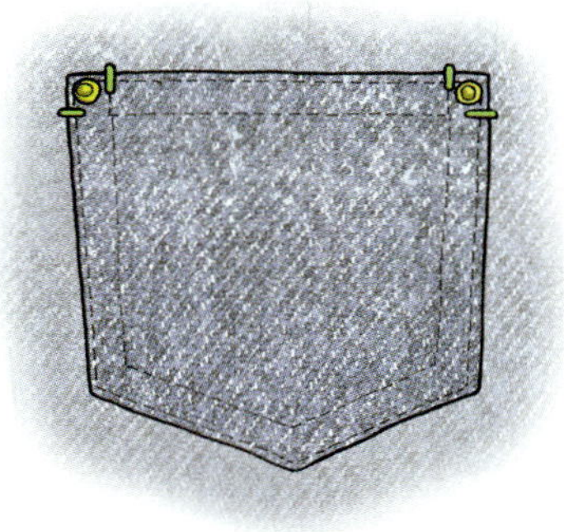

7. Position jean pockets at an angle as shown and top-stitch in place. Use Jean-a-ma-jig to get around rivets.

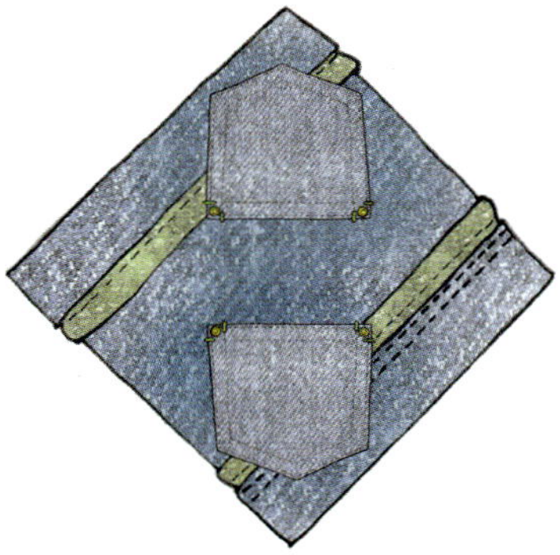

finished pillow
side 1

8. Place left-over mitered corners approximately 1" from the raw edge on all 4 sides of the yellow fabric with points towards center. Position to your liking. Topstitch bias or tubular binding over raw edges all the way around the mitered pieces.

9. Place jeans square and yellow square right sides together. Stitch leaving an 8" opening in the center of one side. Turn inside out and press. Insert pillow form or stuff with fiberfill. Be sure to fill the corners. Close opening with hand stitches or face edges together and stitch by machine.

finished pillow
side 2

10. Finish by pulling shank button through center from both sides creating tuft. Refer to diagram.

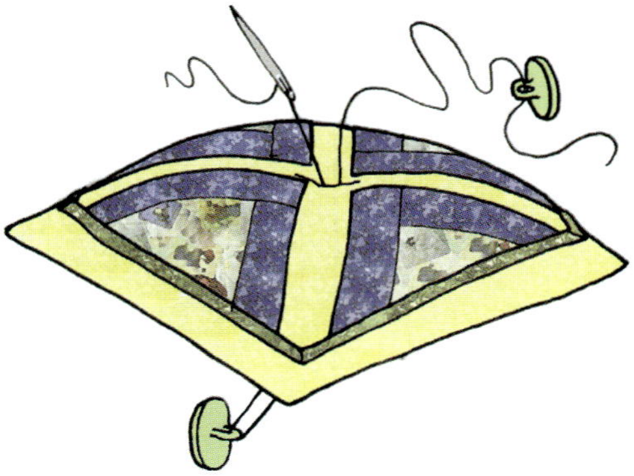

Pockets on Point

Pockets on Point

Rustic, old west and a bit of heart describe these blocks turned on point. Inspiration came when the earthy colors and my background growing up on a ranch just seemed to go together. The challenge of trying to squeeze blocks from every part of the jean proved rewarding. Piecing is required on some of the blocks which allows the character of the jeans to come alive. As I snuggle beneath this quilt, I recount the many times I rode horseback with My Dad. This quilt definitely has personality!

Materials:

- 1 pair gold adult jeans
- 1 pair tan adult jeans
- 1 pair brown adult jeans
- 5-7 pairs blue adult jeans
- 6 similar in kind pockets
- 7/8 yard tan corduroy
- 1/4 yard fusible web
- 1 6" x 6" square gold ultrasuede
- 1 6" x 6" square brown ultrasuede
- 1 6" x 6" square rust ultrasuede
- 9 yards backing fabric (this is for length wise border print)
- 6 yard backing fabric (if not using directional print)
- 1 queen size quilt batting 90" x 108"
- 1 2" Button

Approximate Finished Size: 77" x 102"

Cut:

1. Cut 44 blocks 9 1/2" square from blue jeans

Cut 10 blocks 9 1/2" square from gold jeans

Cut 10 blocks 9 1/2" square from tan jeans

Cut 10 blocks 9 1/2" square from brown jeans (Some piecing may be required).

Cut 1 - 27 1/2" x 27 1/2" square from corduroy. This is the center of the quilt.

2. Cut borders to accommodate lengthwise border fabric. My border print was 7" wide and cut lengthwise the length of quilt.

If you cut border selvage to selvage piecing will be required. I suggest 6 1/2" wide and you will need 8 strips.

3. Trace hearts or cowboy hats provided on fusible web. Press fusible web to gold, rust and brown ultrasuede. Cut around shape and remove paper backing.

Sew:

4. Arrange appliqués and six jean pockets as shown. Fuse appliqués and pin pockets securely. Stitch around pockets and zigzag or use decorative stitch to attach hearts. I used stitch #84 and #85 on the Janome Memory Craft 10000.

Pockets on Point continued

5. Lay out quilt blocks according to diagram and assemble rows in quadrants.

6. The blocks at outer quilt edge *will not line up* and will be trimmed later.

7. Press **ALL** seams away from blue blocks.

8. Stitch lower left quadrant to one side of corduroy. Stitch upper right quadrant to opposite side of corduroy.

9. Stitch or serge upper left quadrant, then lower right.

10. Lay quilt top flat and carefully cut off triangles at quilt edges. You should have a 1/4" seam allowance remaining to stitch borders to.

11. Attach borders along both sides by stitching or serging. **NOTE:** If using a border print or directional fabric make sure the direction is correct.

12. Sew borders across top and bottom of quilt. Piece backing fabric right sides together and stitch length of quilt.

13. Layer batting, quilt top, and backing. Backing and top should be right sides together with batting on the bottom. Stitch around entire quilt, leaving a 12" opening at top edge.

14. Turn inside out like a gigantic pillow. Be patient it will eventually turn.

15. Hand stitch opening and stitch in the ditch around border. To finish, bar tack at corners of every block or tie with yarn or floss.

OPTION: Use heart or hat for stencil design for free motion quilting.

Congratulations! This calls for a snack break.

Pattern Templates:

Trace one of these pattern pieces onto fusible web, and cut 2 of each color.

NOTE:
Denim has a tendency to stretch even more than regular fabric. Make sure the top of the quilt is stretched tightly as you pin to the backing and batting.

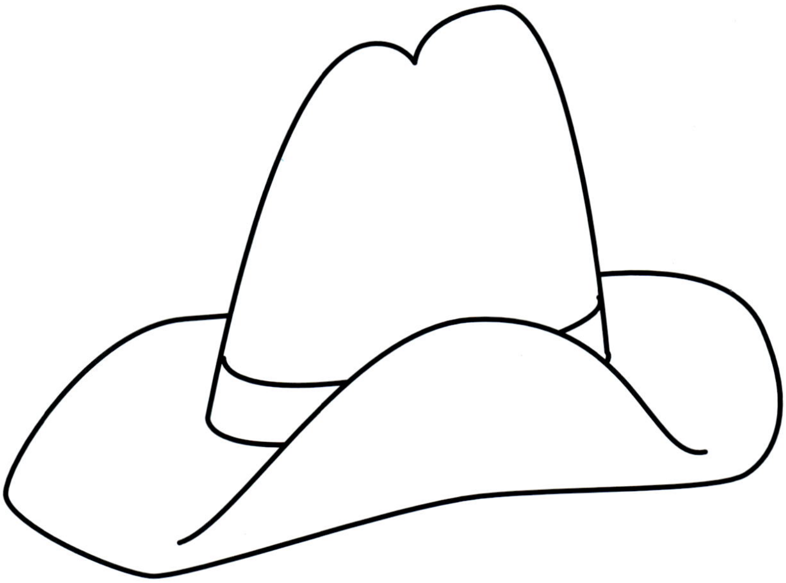

I learned through experience that blocks on the edge should not be trimmed to size before quilt assembly or you will lose the point of the adjoining block. I was trying to save time cutting out so many blue blocks but the extra effort was worth it. Now we have the leftover triangles to create something else! What about pillow shams?

Cornered Tulips

Cornered Tulips came from all the flat felled seams and belt loops I've accumulated from many jean projects. The wall hanging is brightly colored and multi-bordered. The leaves and tulip heads are appliquéd on a background of black jean legs. The flat felled seams and belt loops automatically form the stems and stamens. You'll love the cheater's way to achieve mitered corners on this beautiful display of tulips! It reminds me all winter of My Mother's beautiful tulips, waiting to peak their heads through the warm, spring soil.

Cornered Tulips

Materials:

1 pair black Jeans adult size
1 pair blue jeans (for seams and belt loops)
2 blue belt loops (you may choose to use 4)
1 yard print for backing
1 yard craft or lightweight batting
1/8 yard black & white check for sashing
1/4 yard green for leaves
1/8 yard pink
1/8 yard yellow
1/8 yard blue
1/8 yard turquoise
1/2 yard fusible web
1/2 yard fusible interfacing
1 1" button for middle
8 triangular buttons for sashing

Approximate Finished Size: 29" x 29"

Cut:

1. Cut four 12" squares from black jeans legs. Refer to cutting diagram.

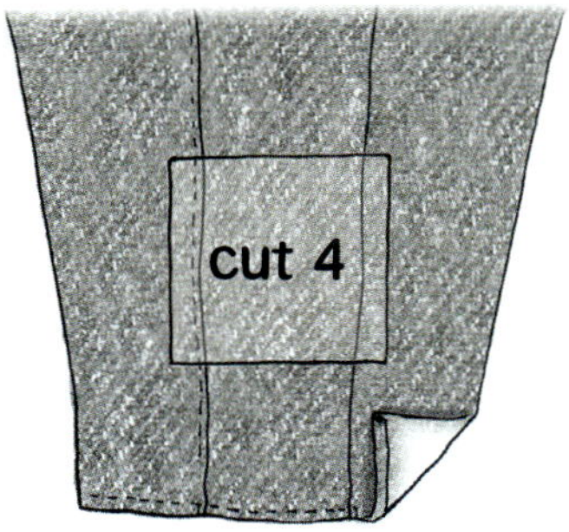

2. Cut or tear one strip 2 1/2" wide from pink, yellow, blue, & turquoise.

3. Cut two strips 2 1/2" wide (or use check for guide) from checked fabric.

4. Cut along both sides of **blue** jean flat felled side seams to use for stems. I used a pinking shear for interest but a plain edge works as well.

5. Remove two belt loops from waistband.

6. Fuse interfacing to wrong side of tulip fabric and green leaf fabric. Use adequate amount and save the rest for the borders.

7. Trace 4 tulips and 4 sets of leaves on fusible web. (Leaves have a direction so don't forget to mirror image two of them).

8. Press fusible web to the back of interfaced leaves and tulip pieces. Cut around design and remove paper backing.

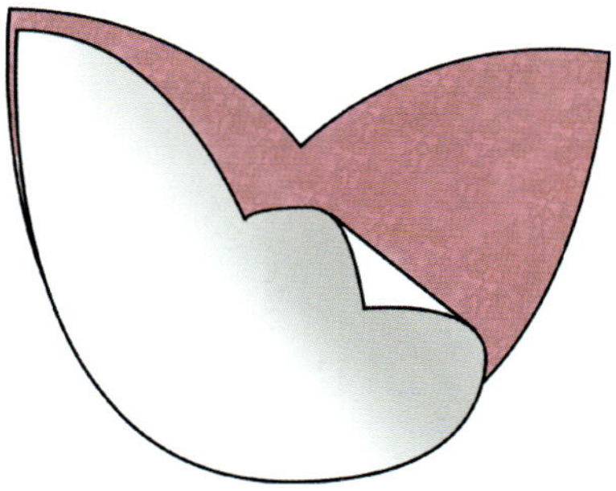

9. Using pattern guide, fuse in place over the flat felled stems and belt loop stamens.

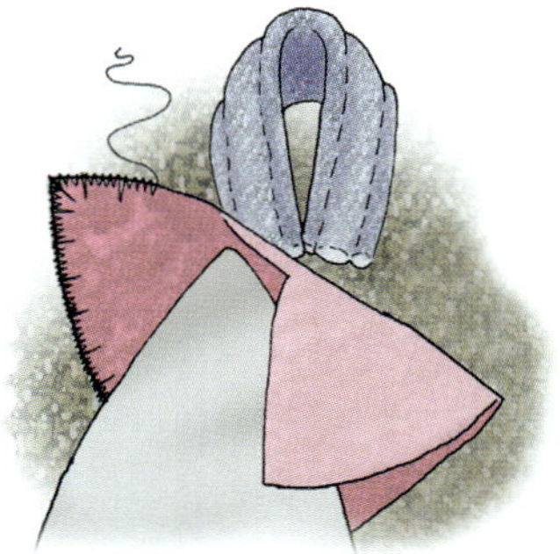

Sew:

10. Stitch down long side of each stem stopping at tulip base. Stem extends freely through middle of tulip on blue and turquoise. By doing this first your appliqué stitches will cover your straight stitching on the stems. Belt loops will be caught in appliqué stitches on the pink and yellow tulips.

Cornered Tulips continued

11. Set machine for small zigzag or appliqué stitch. I used stitches #84 and #85 on the Janome Memory Craft 10000.

12. Stitch around leaves and tulips changing thread color when necessary. **Note:** Do not stitch leaf detail until last. This stitching will go through all layers of the wall hanging.

13. Determine which check color you want in the center of your wall hanging.

14. Sew yellow and turquoise tulip block to checked sashing and cut off excess strip at border edge.

15. Sew blue and pink tulip block to sashing being careful to match checks.

16. Join all four tulip blocks with checked sashing, being careful to match the black and white checks. Cut off excess at border edge.

17. Center and sew yellow border and pink border to opposite sides. **DO NOT** cut off excess yet. Press borders away from wall hanging.

18. Here come the easy miters! Place turquoise border right sides together at edge of tulip block and fold turquoise border at side edge of yellow as shown. Begin stitching in the corner of yellow and turquoise border and continue stitching to the pink stopping at border. Repeat for blue border.

19. Press turquoise away from wall hanging and watch the automatic miters appear. Pin the diagonal corners in place and stitch to the corners on all four corners.

20. Now trim off the excess on the yellow and pink sides. Yea your miters are perfect!

21. Center the wall hanging on top of the batting. Lay the backing fabric right sides together and trim both the batting and the backing fabric to fit wall hanging.

22. Stitch all the way around the outer edge leaving a 6″ opening for turning. Turn inside out and lightly press outer edges.

23. Hand stitch opening with invisible stitches.

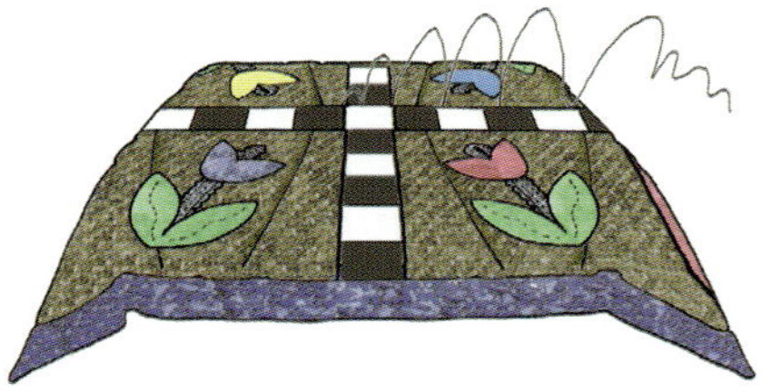

24. Change to your walking foot and holding wall hanging taut, stitch in the ditch around borders, between blocks and around checked sashing.

25. Sew decorative buttons evenly spaced on sashing through all layers. Now for the final touch. Add the detail lines in the middle of the leaves.

Hurray Success!

Pattern Templates

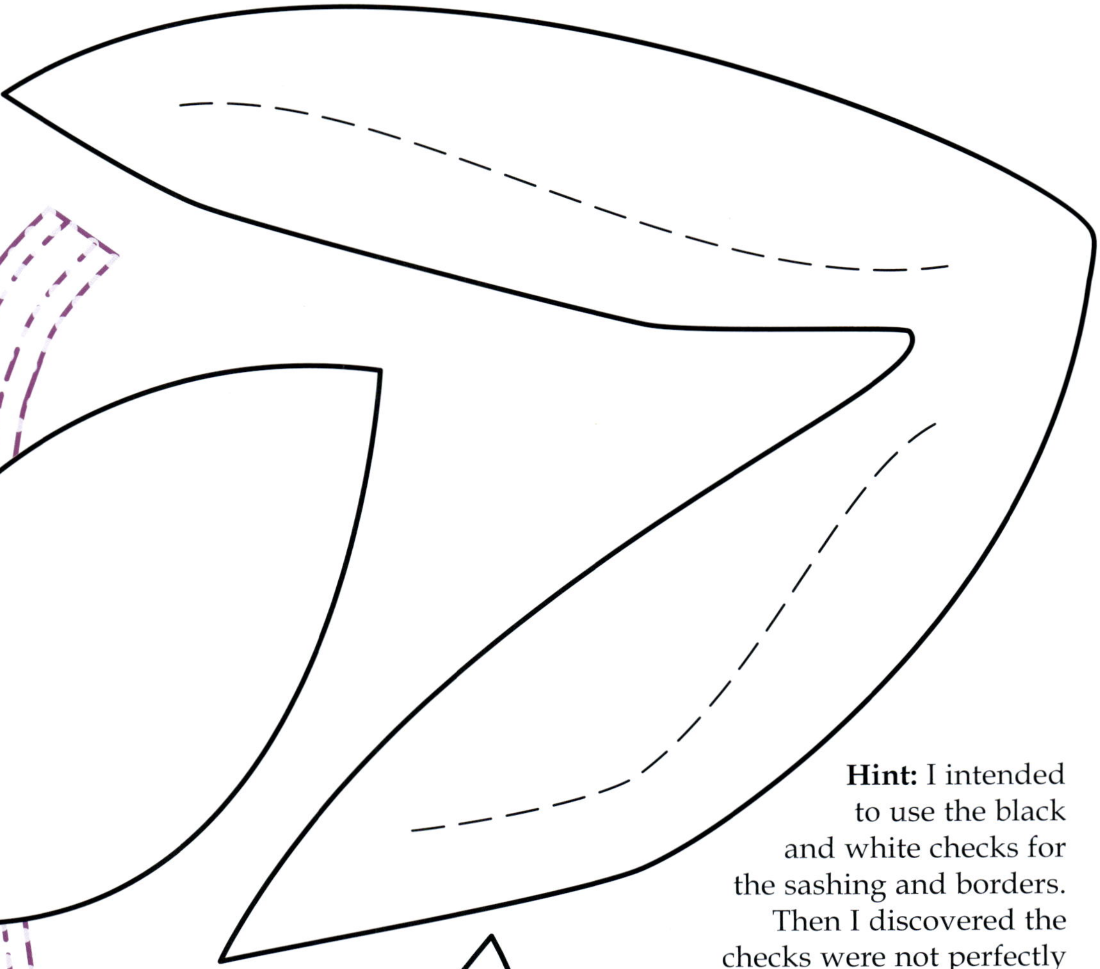

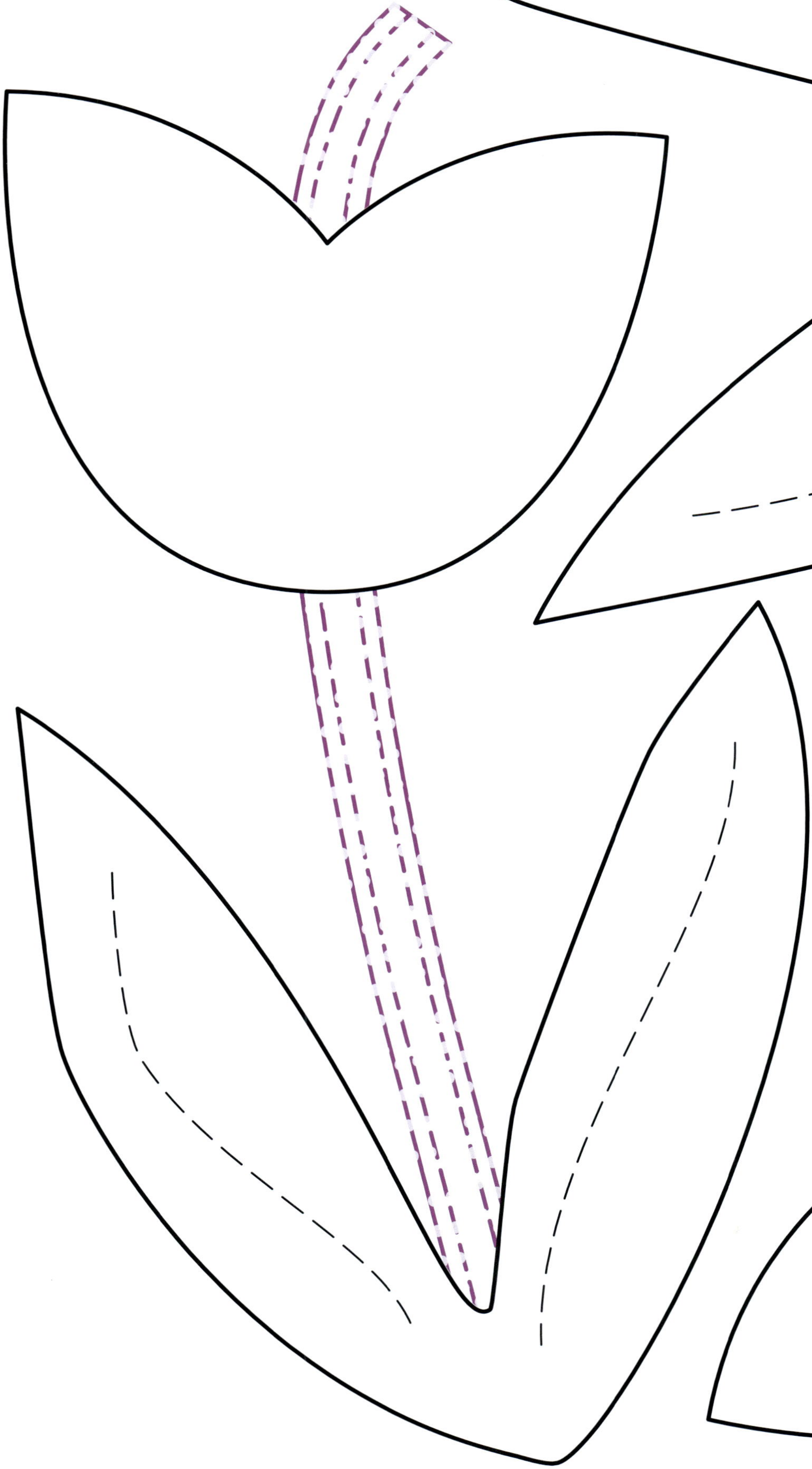

Hint: I intended to use the black and white checks for the sashing and borders. Then I discovered the checks were not perfectly square, making it impossible to match at the border edges and mitered corners. This inspired a different plan and the multi-borders were incorporated to carry out the tulips.

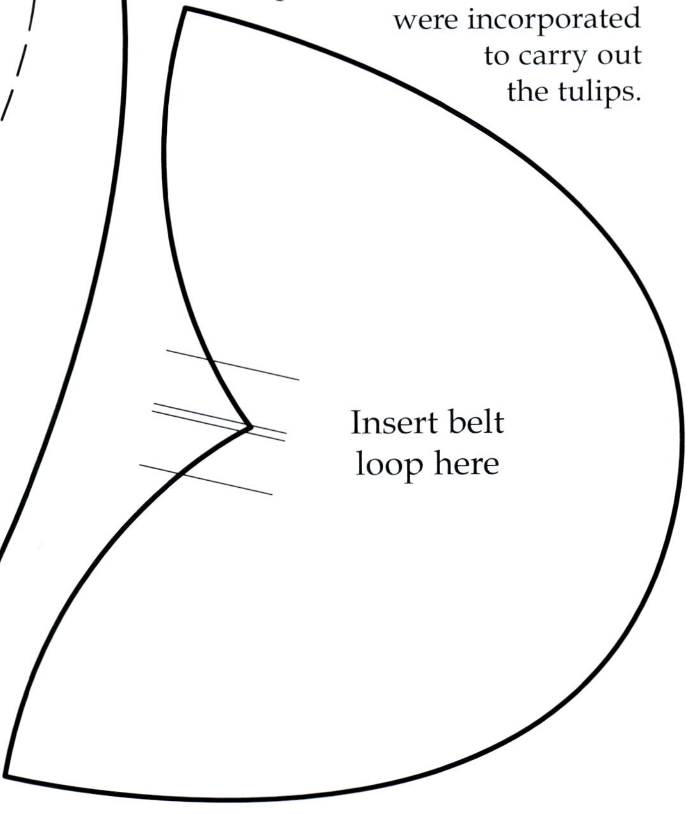

In-Vest In Your Baby

In-Vest In Your Baby

The kids are grown and out of the house and you're left with their old blue jeans. Why not preserve your son's or daughter's favorite pair by making this adorable baby quilt? Proud parents can bring home their newborn wrapped in recycled remnants from favorite jeans and Grandma's diaper pins.

Materials:

1 large jean pocket
1 pair blue jeans any size
¾ yard white eyelet
¾ yard fusible interfacing
¼ yard blue
¼ yard pink
¼ yard yellow
½ yard pink dot for border
1⅛ yard backing
1¼ yard quilt batting
1 yard white eyelet trim
9 diaper pins
1 package pink baby rick rack
1 package satin blanket binding

Approximate Finished Size: 38" x 38"

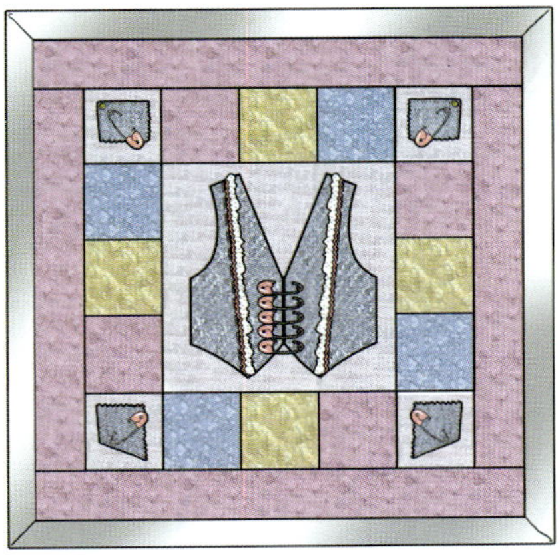

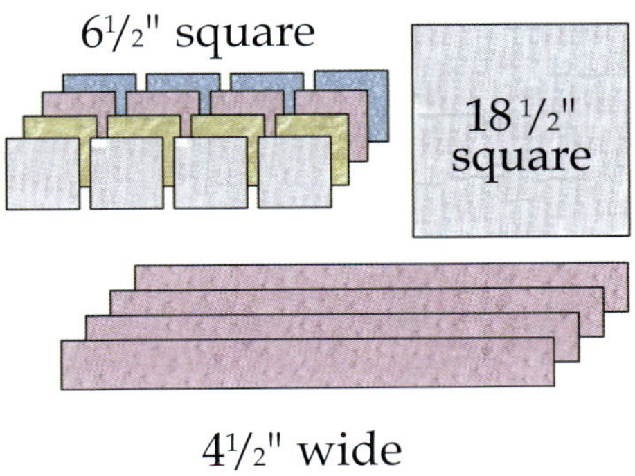

Cut 4 - 4½" wide strips, selvage to selvage, from pink dot for border

Prepare:

1. Press fusible interfacing to wrong side of white eyelet

Cut:

2. Cut 1 - 18½" x 18½" square from white eyelet fabric

Cut 4 - 6½" squares from blue, pink, yellow, & white eyelet

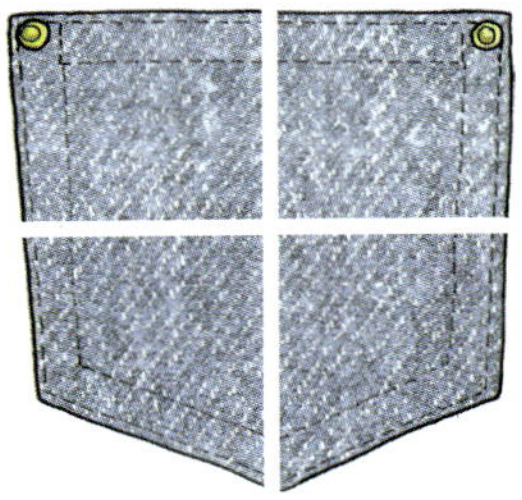

Cut large jean pocket into quarters as shown.

3. Cut vest front pieces from jean legs according to layout. Wash and press with spray starch.

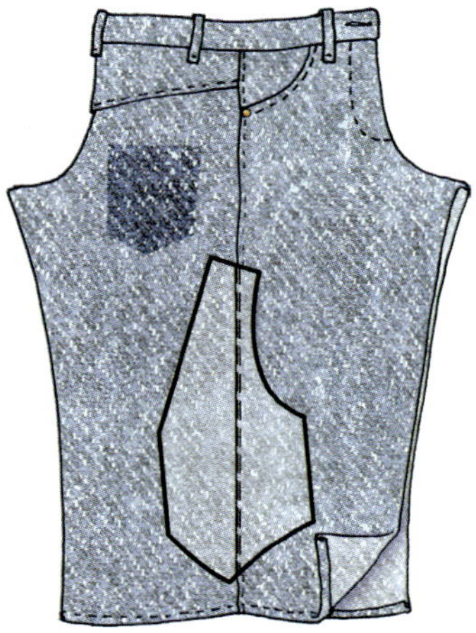

In-Vest In Your Baby continued

Sew:

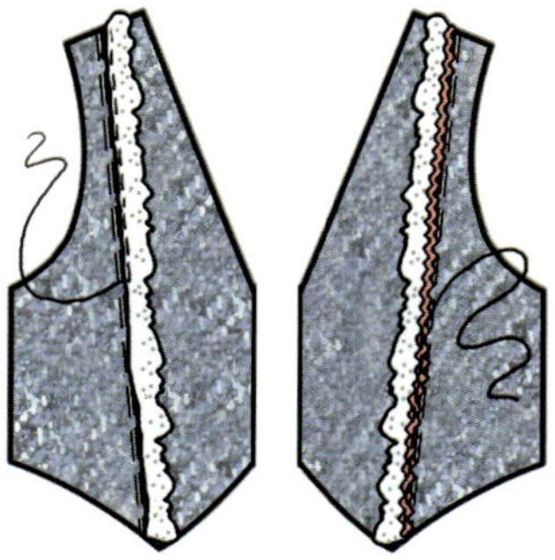

4. Stitch white eyelet trim beside flat felled seam on vest front. Stitch pink baby rick rack over white eyelet trim. See picture. Lay these two jean pieces aside.

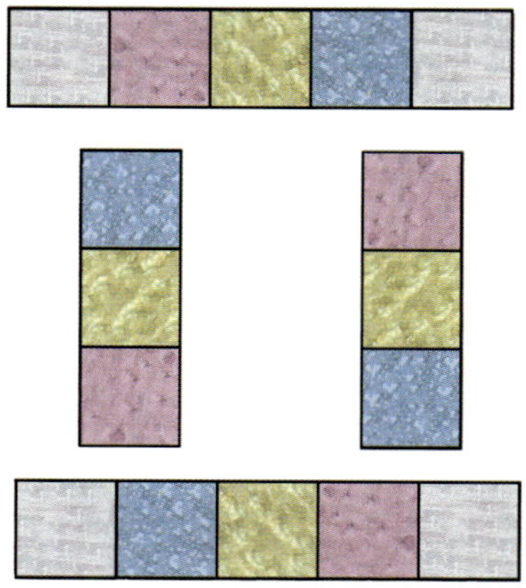

5. Assemble and stitch 4 sets of pink, yellow, and blue squares.

6. Stitch white eyelet blocks to both ends of two sets.

7. Sew pink, yellow and blue blocks to each side of 18 1/2" white eyelet center piece. Stitch pink, yellow, blue and white eyelet blocks across other two sides.

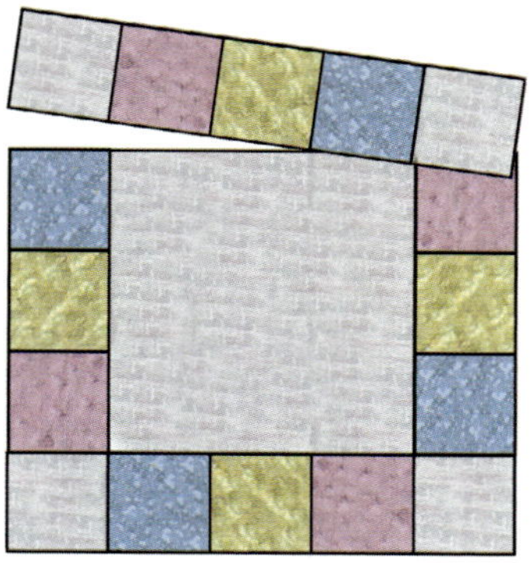

8. Add 4 1/2" pink dot border to all four sides, alternating opposite sides as you go.

9. Layer backing wrong side up, then batting, and quilt top. Trim raw edges of all layers evenly.

10. Encase raw edge with satin blanket binding and pin securely folding out fullness at corners.

11. Change to walking foot. (Optional)

12. Lengthen stitch length and choose wide zigzag to stitch through all layers around all 4 edges of quilt.

NOTE: I like to piece binding in the corner so it's camouflaged by the folded miter.

13. Stitch in the ditch around blocks.

14. Now to decorate: Position vest front pieces in center of eyelet square and stitch through all layers. (You are machine quilting this project as you go). Stitch additional lines along flat felled seam on vest front piece.

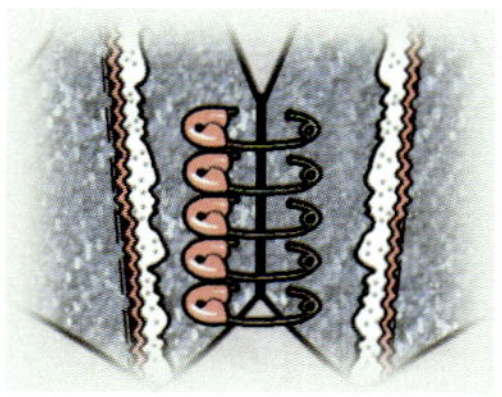

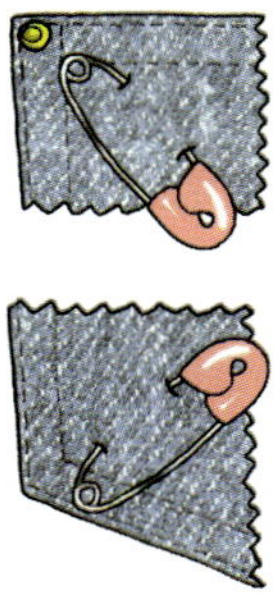

15. Topstitch quartered adult jeans pocket to corner of white eyelet blocks. Decorate with diaper pins.

16. Pin diaper pins across vest fronts.

Hint: If you have trouble finding just the right color of old-fashioned diaper pins try this: Get out your favorite color of nail polish and paint the diaper pin heads to your liking!

Pattern Templates

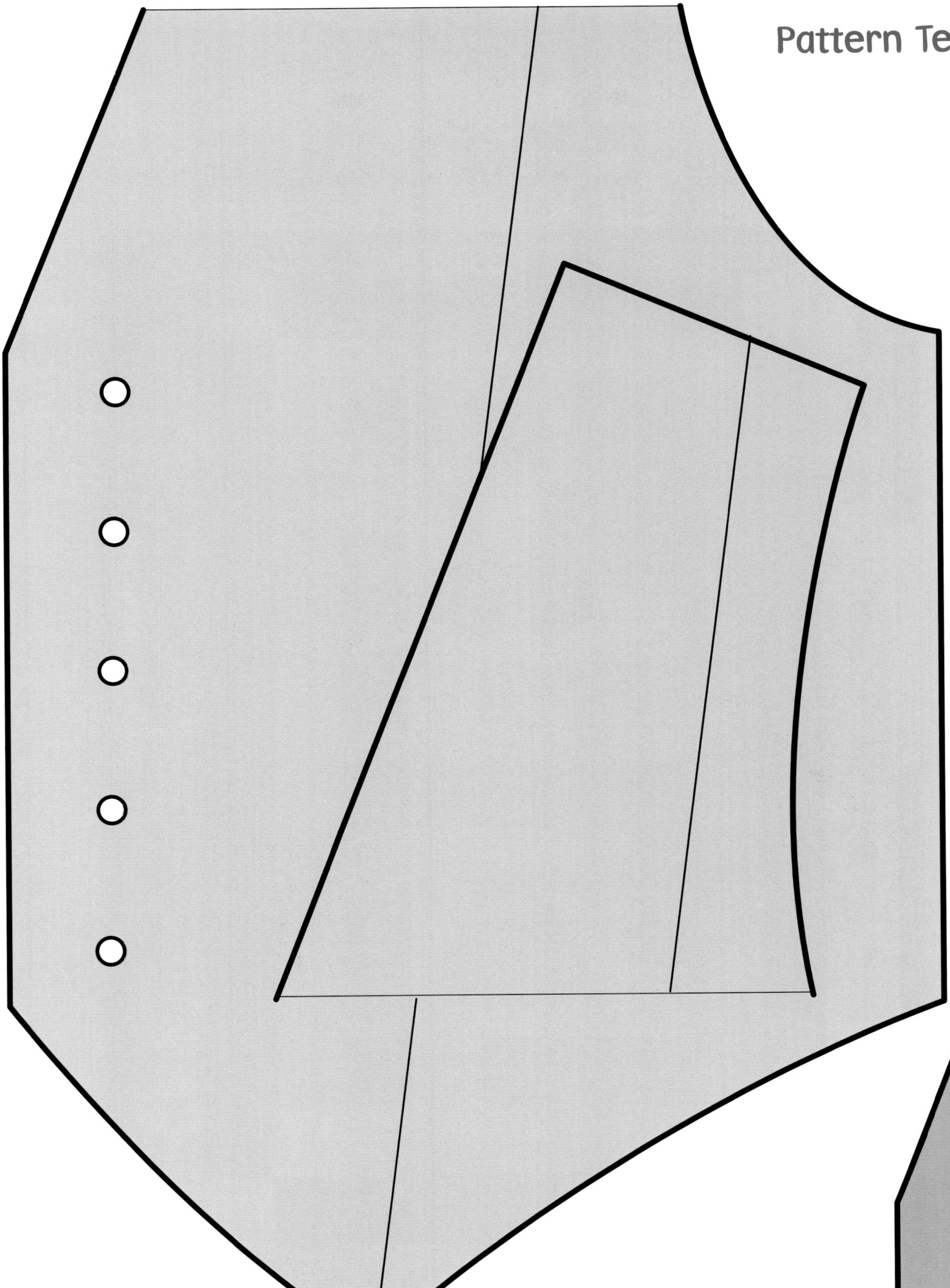

Sweet Dreams!

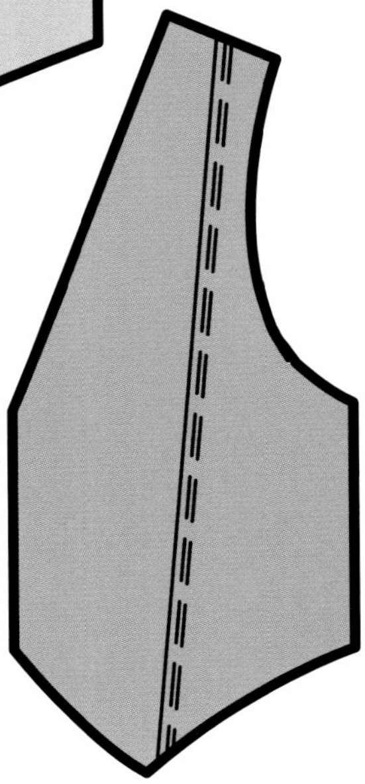

A-B-C Kid's Quilt

A-B-C Kid's Quilt

Children will love learning the A, B, C's when at play on top of this colorful quilt. It is an enlarged version of the Baby Quilt from the previous pages. It features Jean pockets on the side borders to keep their treasures close at hand. Shades of blue compose the lettered blocks and Jean legs are used to preserve that favorite pair of denims. This quilt will have many stories to tell as it is passed from one toddler to the next.

Materials:

- 2 pairs light blue adult jeans (I used wrong side of denim for shade variation)
- 2 pairs medium blue adult jeans
- 2 pairs dark blue adult jeans
- 10 jean pockets (for borders)
- $1\frac{1}{2}$ yard yellow (centers and corner blocks)
- $1\frac{1}{2}$ yard red dot
- $7\frac{1}{2}$ yard teddy bear print (border and backing)
- $1\frac{1}{4}$ yard blue & white stripe
- $\frac{3}{4}$ yard fusible web
- Quilt batting at least 68" x 102"
- 1 package red baby rick rack
- 4 packages extra wide bias tape
- 16 metal eyelets
- $2\frac{1}{2}$ yards leather lacing or shoe laces

Approximate Finished Size:
66" x 99" (extra long)

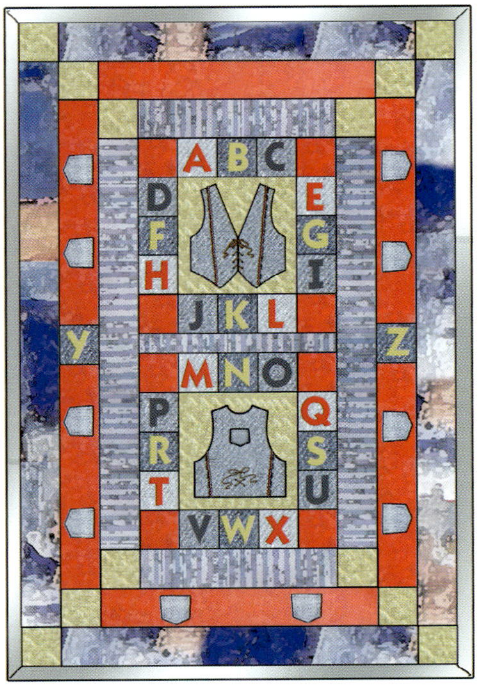

Cut:

1. Cut 8 - 6 1/2" blocks light blue jeans.
Cut 8 - 6 1/2" blocks medium blue jeans.
Cut 10 - 6 1/2" blocks dark blue jeans.

2. Cut 2 - 18 1/2" X 18 1/2" square yellow.
Cut 12 - 6 1/2" blocks yellow.
Cut 1 - 3" strip (for sashing) blue & white stripe.
Cut 6 - 6 1/2" strips blue & white stripe selvage to selvage.
Cut 8 - 6 1/2" blocks red dot.
Cut 6 - 6 1/2" strips red dot selvage to selvage.
Cut 8 - 6 1/2" strips teddy bear print

A-B-C Kid's Quilt continued

3. Cut vest front and back from jean legs. Wash vest pieces and press with spray starch. Zigzag rick rack along flat felled seam on both fronts and back.

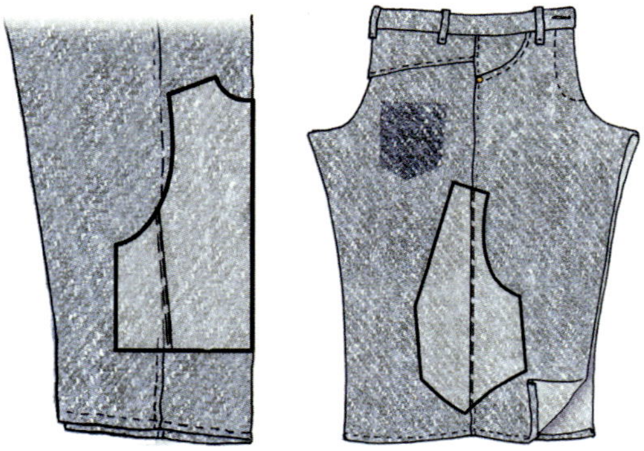

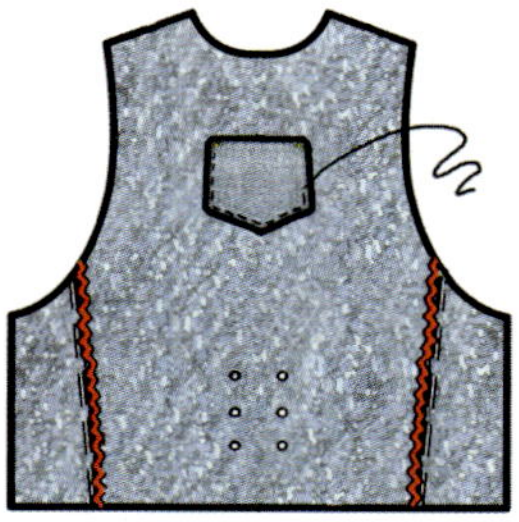

Topstitch watch pocket to back piece. Bar tack beside the rivets in watch pocket.

4. Punch holes down front edges and in back piece for eyelets. Insert eyelets and squeeze with snap pliers. **Option:** You can make buttonholes if you do not have eyelet pliers. Using Space-Tape™ with pre-determined buttonholes makes this easy.

Sew

5. Center vest pieces on yellow center squares and topstitch around raw edges of vest fronts and back.

6. Trace letters provided on fusible web. Press web to wrong side of denim scraps. Cut around letters and remove paper backing. Press alphabet to center of denim blocks using the photo or diagram for guide. (Experiment with fabric scraps for your alphabet). Zigzag around letters using different colored thread.

7. In the denim A, B, C Quilt shown, I used Janome memory card #108 on the Memory Craft 9000. This card features appliqué and monogram designs.

8. Arrange lettered blocks as shown and stitch on both edges of both yellow squares. Stitch red corner blocks to remaining alphabet and stitch to top and bottom on both yellow squares. **Y** and **Z** will be used later in the border.

9. Join the two sections of quilt together with 3" striped sashing. Trim excess strip at edge to fit.

10. Piece striped border and stitch to both long edges of quilt. Stitch yellow corner blocks to top and bottom striped borders.

11. Pin striped border to top and bottom edge of quilt and stitch. **HINT:** I like to attach one corner block at a time and measure border strips to top and bottom edge. Cut off excess border and sew opposite corner block to assure a correct fit.

12. Stitch red border strips to top and bottom of **Y** and **Z** blocks. Center **Y** and **Z** on long edges of quilt and stitch, trimming excess border at top and bottom of quilt.

13. Stitch yellow corner blocks to remaining red border and stitch across top and bottom. **NOTE:** Yellow corner blocks should meet at corners.

14. Piece strips together for final border. Sew teddy bear border to long edges of quilt and trim to fit.

15. Stitch yellow corner blocks to remaining teddy bear border and stitch to top and bottom. Yellow corner blocks should match at corners.

16. This quilt was quilted on a Handi Quilter™. Handi Quilter™ is a framework that allows you to use **your** machine for free-form quilting. The quilt is pinned in place to fabric leaders and using your sewing machine you quilt through all layers as you go.

17. The edges of this quilt were encased with extra wide double fold bias tape. A wide zigzag was used to catch both edges of tape at once.

18. If using a traditional method of finishing follow the directions on page 22. for layering fabric and turning. Stitch in the ditch or tie through all layers of your quilt.

19. Sew pockets to red border through all layers. This final stitching will give borders additional quilting detail.

Have fun teaching your toddler the A, B, C's.

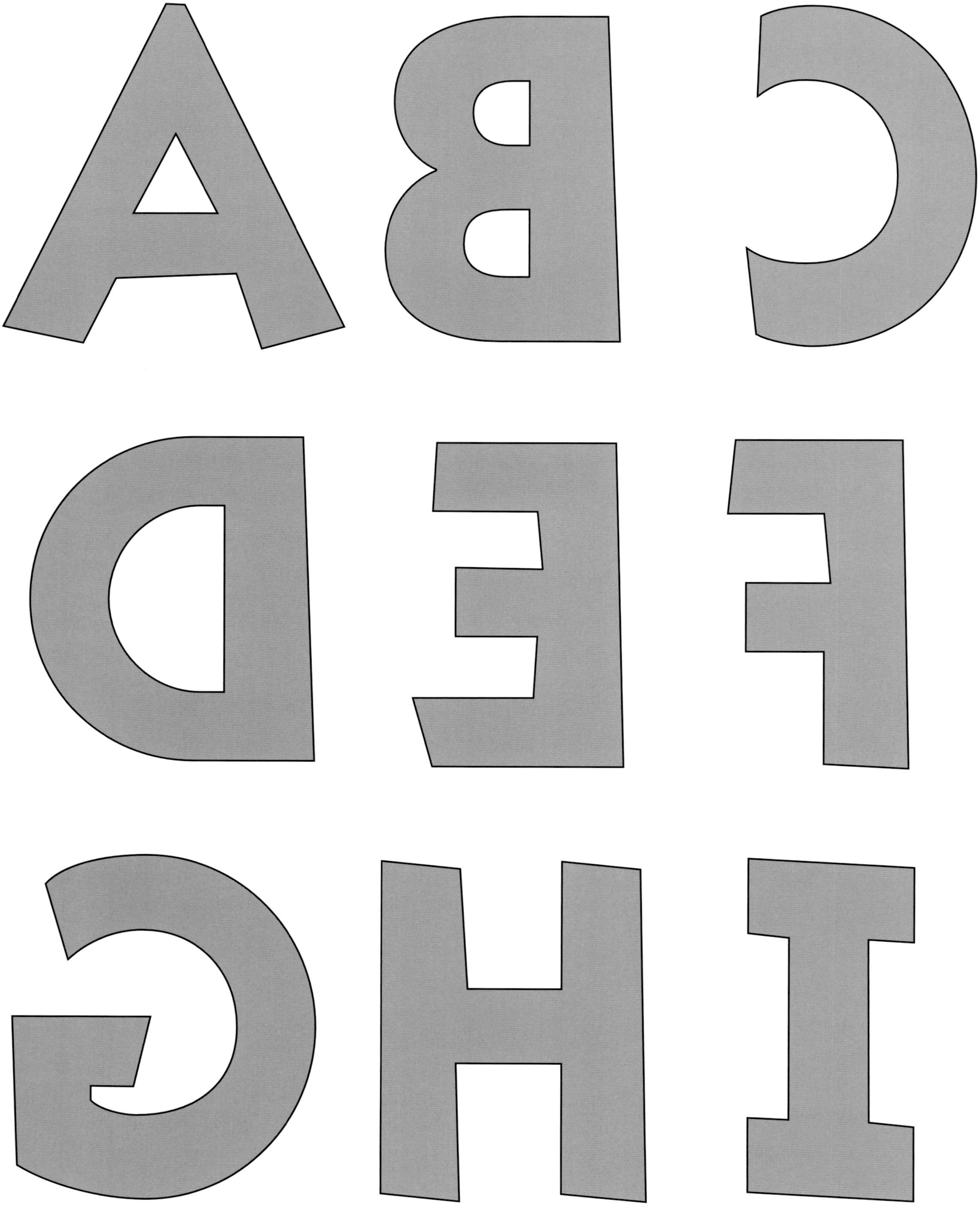
A B C
D E F
G H I

J K L
M N O
P Q R

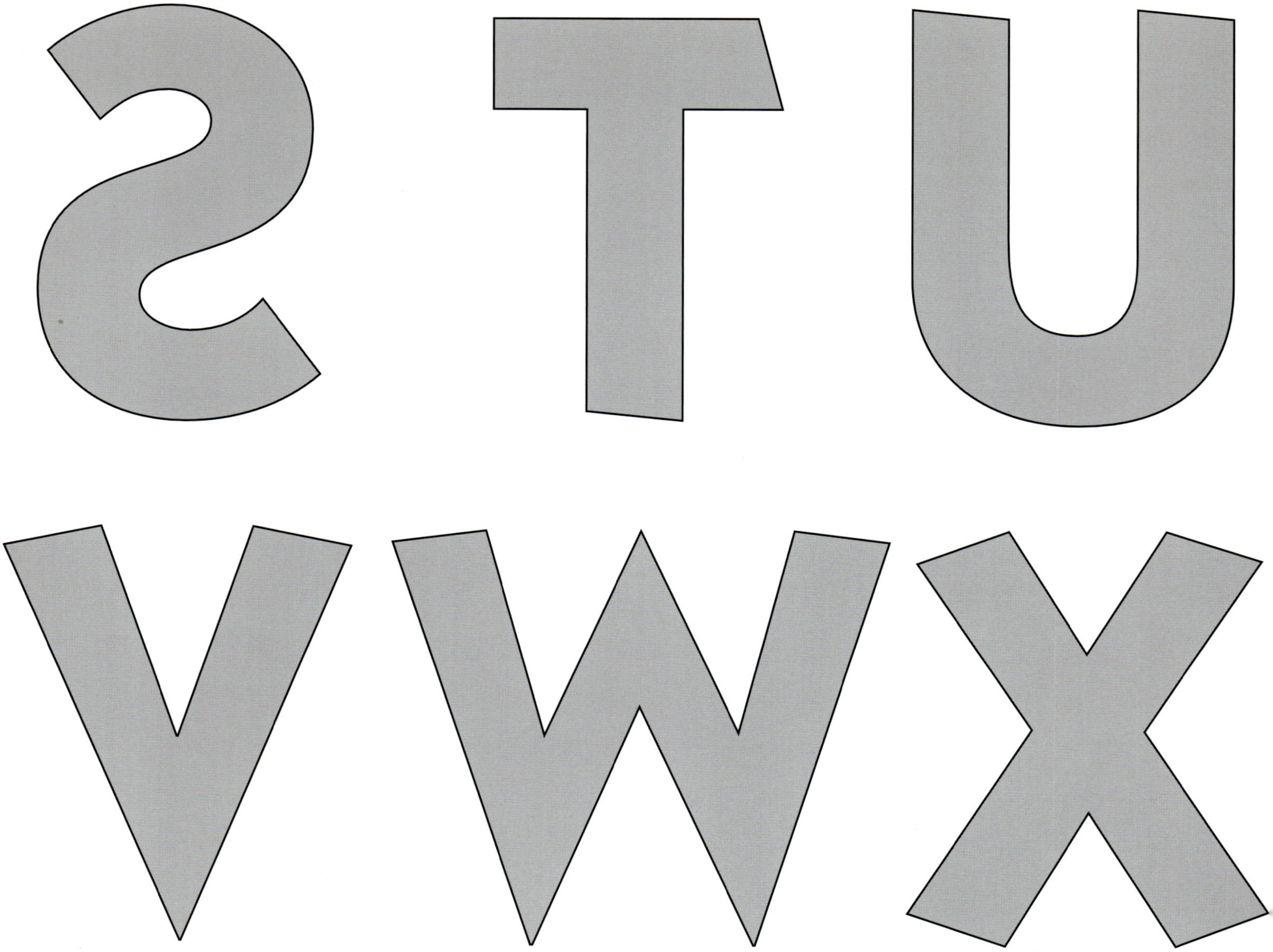

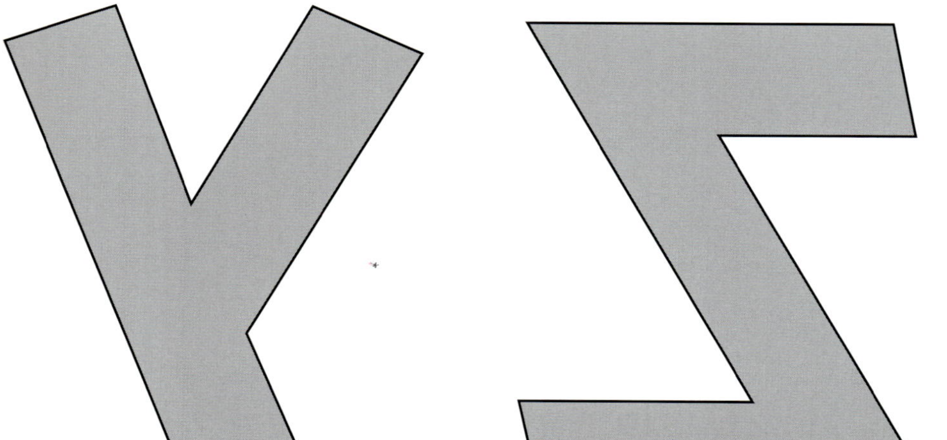

Try appliquéing the complete alphabet on one piece of fabric. Then cut around blocks centering the letters using View & Do Shapes™ from Kaye Wood Inc. There are different shapes in different sizes to view your alphabet or other fussy cut projects to achieve perfect centering.

Pattern Templates

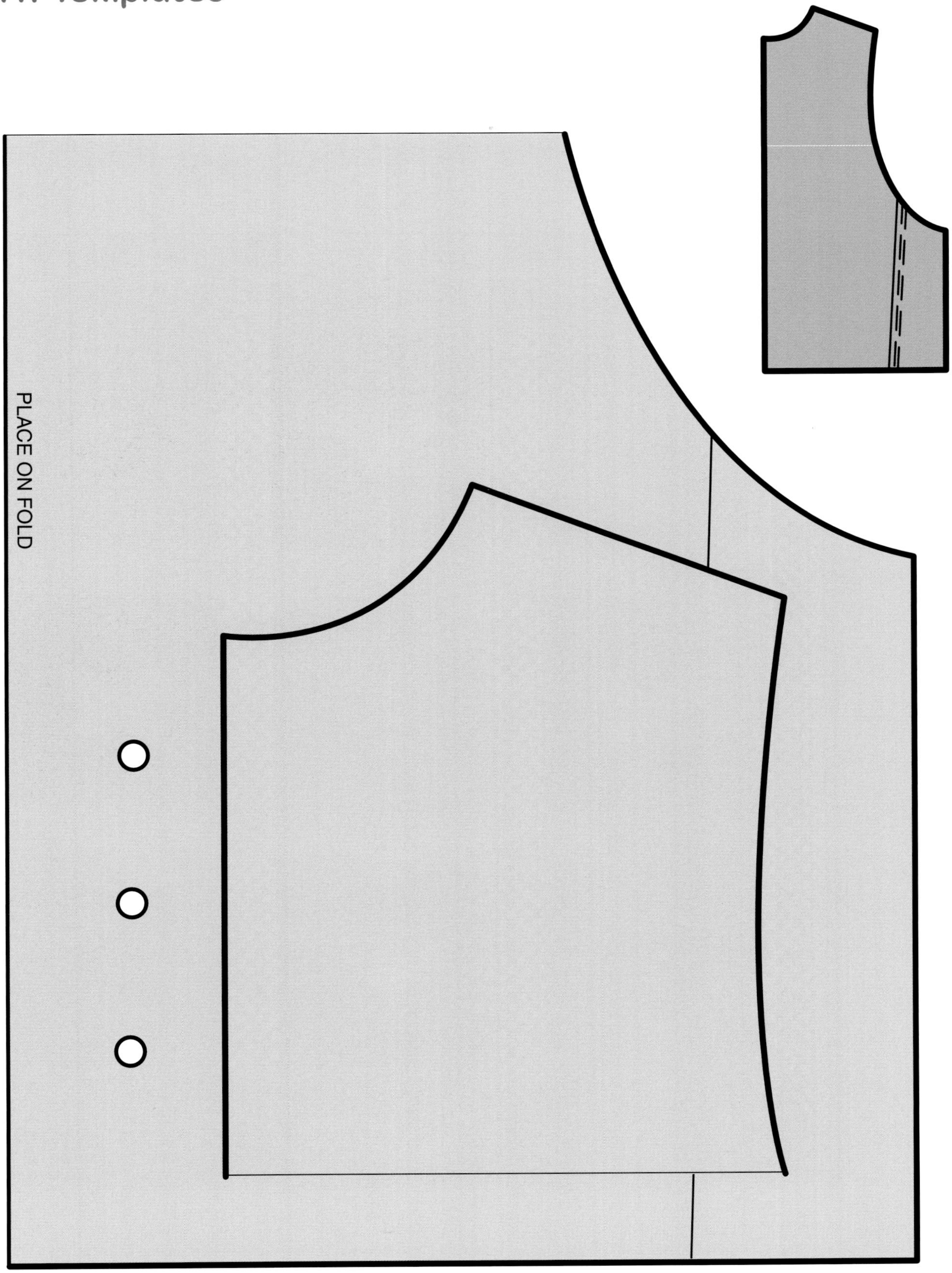

Fly-Front Butterflies and Shoulder Pads

Fly-Front Butterflies and Shoulder Pads

This butterfly wall hanging is truly a recycling experience. I delight in creating **Something** from **Nothing**. So gather a broken zipper, shoulder pads, and two contrasting pairs of your Junk Jeans to come up with this quilted wall hanging that appears to take flight on its own. I chose a butterfly print for the backing so I could carry the motif to the front for appliqués. These butterflies are featured in bold electric colors but imagine using soft pastels as spring comes to life.

Materials:

1 pair black adult jeans
1 pair royal blue adult jeans
4 black shoulder pads
1/4 yard fusible interfacing
1/4 yard fusible web
1/4 yard black lace or netting
3/8 yard multi-print
3/8 yard black and white check
1 1/2 yard backing fabric (extra allowed for appliqués)
48 multi-colored seed beads or perhaps assorted pearls
36" x 36" thin batting
Approximate Finished Size: 35" x 35"

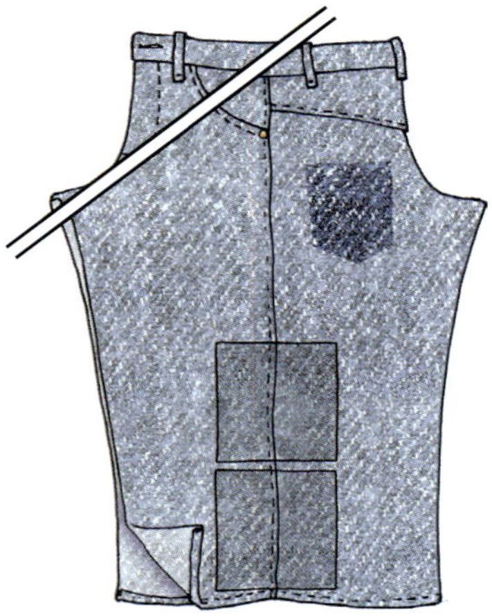

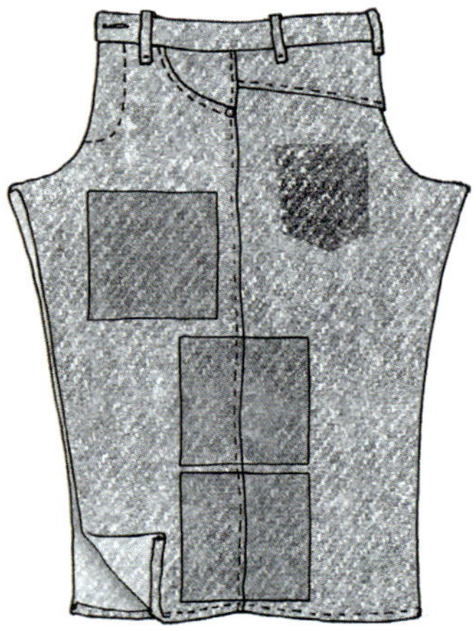

Cut:

1. Cut 4 - 9 1/2" royal blue squares on side seam of leg as shown.

Cut 4 - 9 1/2" black squares on side seam of leg as shown.

Cut 1 - 9 1/2" black square from jeans with no side seam.

Cut or tear 4 - 2 1/2" strips from black and white check selvage to selvage.

2. Cut or tear 4 - 2 1/2" strips from multi-print selvage to selvage. Cut fly front away from jeans as diagramed. You must break zipper to achieve this cut.

HINT: I like to cut extra large then position on block and trim to fit.

3. Choose 4 designs to use as appliqué from print fabric and rough cut around them. Press fusible interfacing to wrong side.

Fly-Front Butterflies continued

4. Press fusible web to wrong side of interfaced appliqué design. Carefully cut around appliqué shape. Remove paper backing and fuse in place on black blocks.

Sew:

5. Stitch with narrow zigzag or appliqué stitch.

6. Hand embroider butterfly antennae.

7. Prepare shoulder pads by covering them with net or lace. Select scallop stitch or satin stitch and stitch close to curved edge. I used stitch #51 on the Janome Memory Craft 10000.

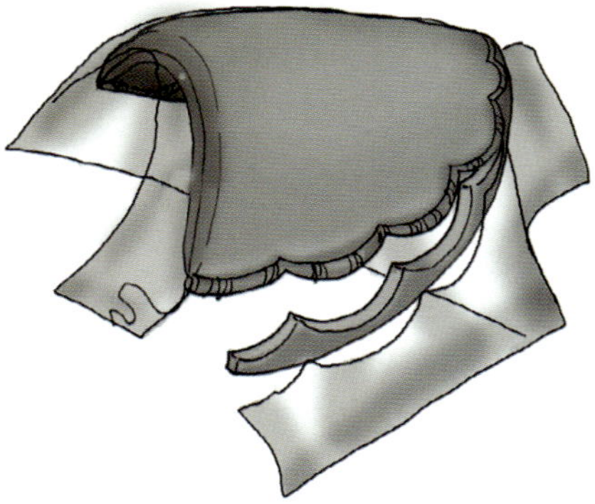

8. Trim lace or net close to stitches. Sew an **"X"** through middle of shoulder pad to define wings.

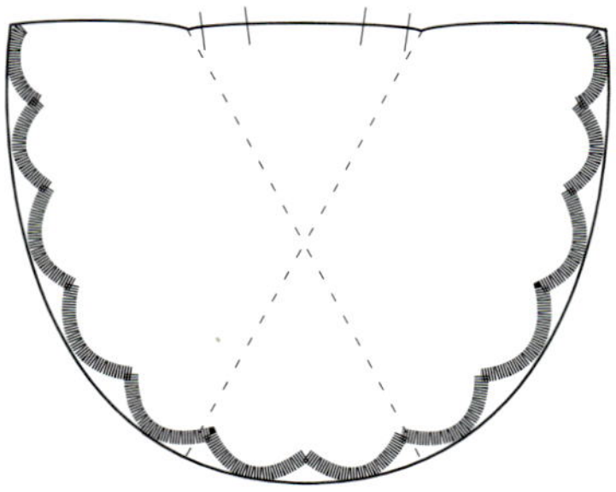

9. Hand stitch beads or pearls to wings.

10. Position 3" of broken zipper teeth on either side of flat felled seam on royal blue blocks. Tack with zigzag at both ends. (This is the shoulder pad butterfly antennae).

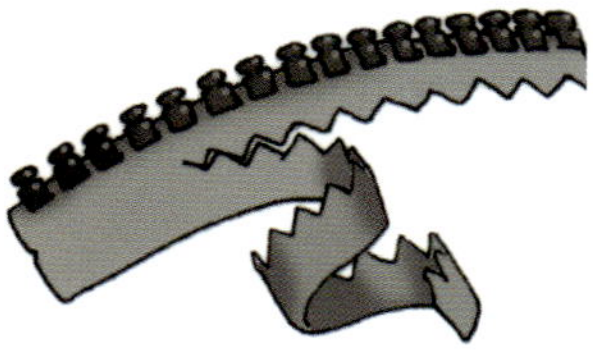

11. Place covered shoulder pads over broken zipper ends (antenna) and stitch with straight stitch around curved edge from wing to wing. Tack straight edge of shoulder pad at base of antenna.

12. Pivot fly front at waistband button or snap. Place fly front from royal blue jeans over center black block and baste at raw edges. Trim fly front to match block.

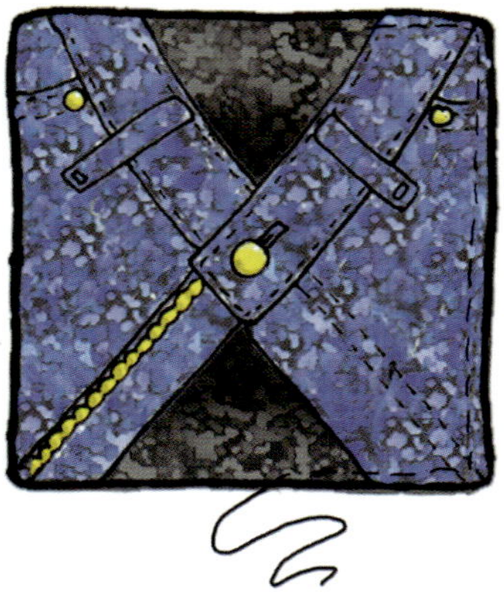

13. Unbutton and appliqué surprise butterfly under fly.

14. Stitch vertical rows as shown with checked sashing.

15. Join rows with multi-colored print, trimming at edges.

16. Stitch checked border at sides only. Do not trim excess.

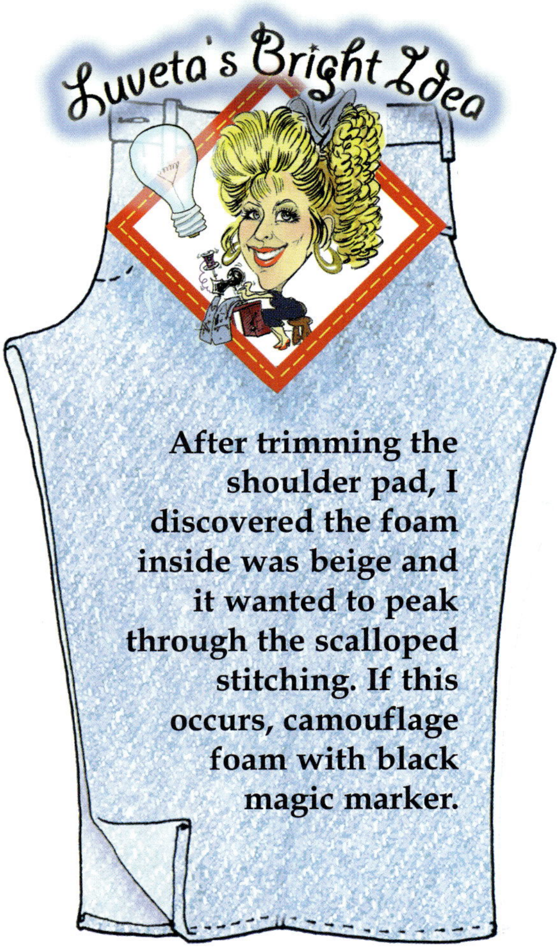

After trimming the shoulder pad, I discovered the foam inside was beige and it wanted to peak through the scalloped stitching. If this occurs, camouflage foam with black magic marker.

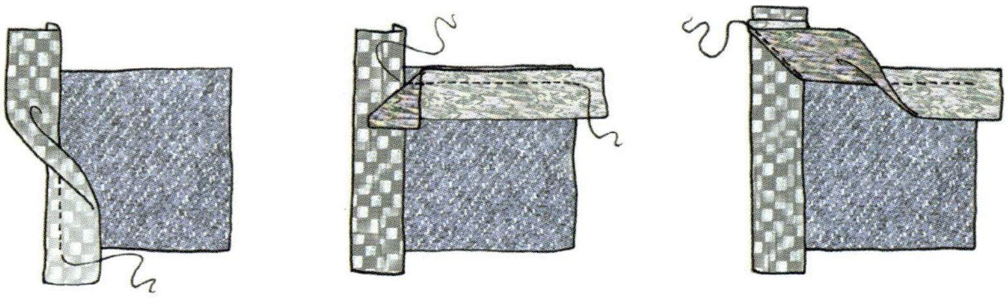

17. Finish the mitered corners the same way as the tulip wall hanging on page 26.

18. Layer batting, wall hanging and backing as shown, leaving an 8 inch opening.

20. Invisibly hand stitch opening.

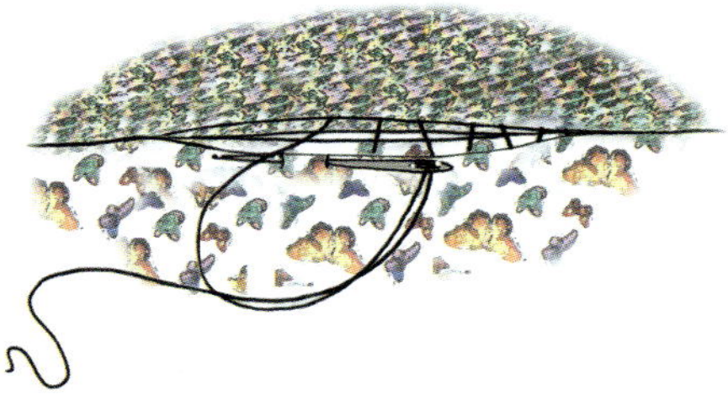

19. Turn inside out.

21. Stitch in the ditch around all blocks through all layers. A walking foot makes this easy to do.

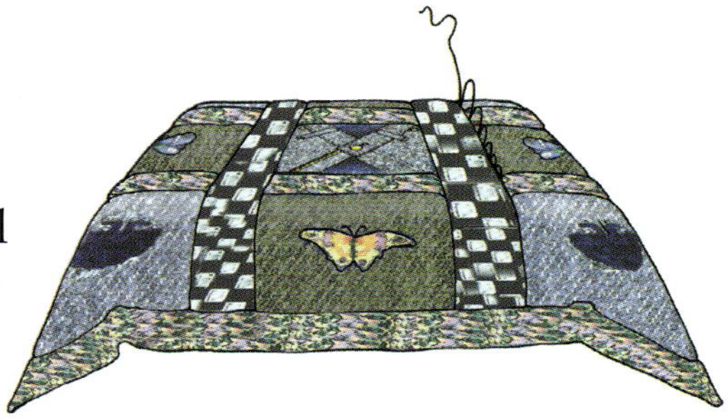

Christmas Card Pockets

Christmas Card Pockets

Christmas cards fit nicely and are kept neatly organized in this Christmas card holder. During the holidays, this wall hanging will bring cheer to any wall or front door. I used bigger pockets to accommodate any size card. Using the alphabet provided, consider changing the message to M – A – I – L and use the vertical pockets year round. A broken wooden pants hanger is recycled for this project.

Materials:

1 pair green adult jeans (or color of your choice)
4 larger blue jean pockets
3 belt loops
3 1/2 yard green cording
1 1/2 yard Christmas print
1/2 yard red dot
1 1/2 yard red cord for hanging
1/4 yard fusible web
1/4 yard fusible interfacing
16 jingle bells
22" x 50" craft batting
Broken wooden pants hanger or 16" of 1/4" dowel
Approximate Finished Size: 21" x 48"

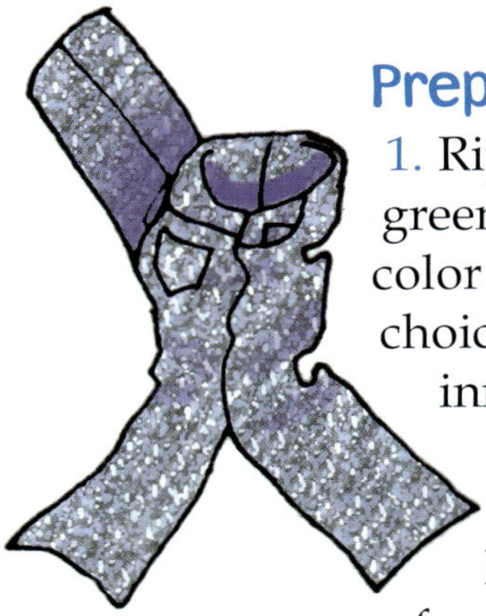

Prepare:

1. Rip or tear green jeans (or color of your choice) at inner leg seam on right leg. Rip front crotch to bottom of zipper. Remove metal stop with pliers and break zipper. (I like to leave the zipper pull on exposed zipper for character).

2. Carefully remove a few stitches at side seam hem and rip to waistline. Cut through waistband.

NOTE: Only 1/4 of the green jeans are used. You will have enough for three more Christmas card holders or you can save the jean sections for another project.

3. Press flat and lay aside.

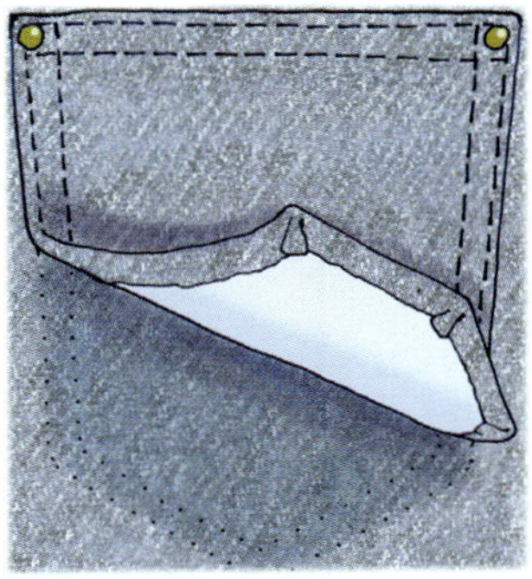

4. Remove pockets from 2 pairs of blue jeans using utility knife.

5. Press fusible interfacing to wrong side of red dot fabric using just enough for letters.

6. Trace N – O – E – L on fusible web.

7. Fuse to wrong side of interfaced red dot.

Christmas Card Pockets continued

Cut:

8. Cut out the letters and remove paper backing of fusible web.

9. Fuse letters in place in center of blue jean pockets.

10. Appliqué around letters using decorative stitch or narrow zigzag.

11. Cut Christmas fabric 16" x 44".

12. Cut three borders 3" wide selvage to selvage from red dot.

Sew:

13. Sew border right sides together along both sides of Christmas print.

14. Stitch remaining 3" border to top and bottom, trimming excess border to fit.

15. Position Christmas fabric with red border on top of the batting, being sure to center it.

16. Cut remaining Christmas fabric to fit for backing and place right sides together.

17. Pin all edges securely and trim off excess batting.

18. Sew around all 4 edges using walking foot, leaving an 8" opening.

19. Turn inside out and pull out corners. Invisibly hand stitch opening.

20. Thread Jingle bells on green cording. Starting at lower right corner, place cording at border and zigzag over green cord while evenly spacing jingle bells.

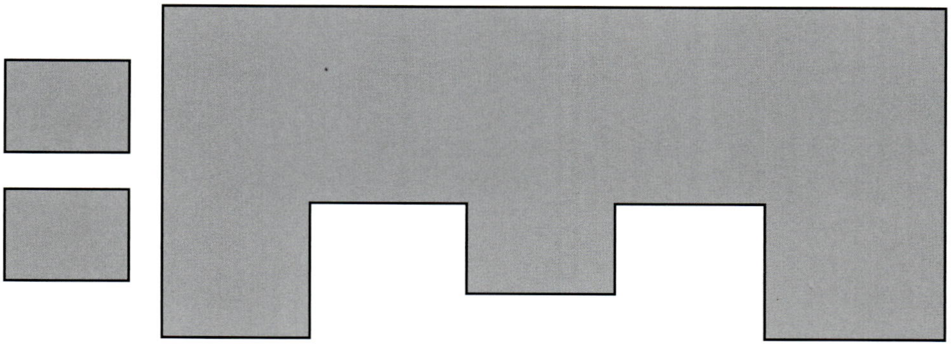

21. Break stitching at jingle bell and continue to zigzag over cord through all layers until all bells are in place. I spaced the bells approximately 7" apart.

22. Hand stitch the last bell to conceal raw edges of cord, meeting in the lower right corner.

23. Position green jean leg in center of Christmas print and zigzag around raw edge being careful at waistband and leaving hem of jean free. (Use Jean-a-ma-jig at belt loop to help level foot and prevent broken needles).

24. Evenly space appliquéd pockets and pin into place. Topstitch through all layers.

25. On the back of the Christmas card holder, position 3 belt loops folded in half at top edge and topstitch as shown.

26. Insert bottom rung of broken wooden pants hanger through the loops. (About 16" long). Or you can use 1/4" dowel stick.

27. Tie red cording to each end of stick and adjust to your liking.

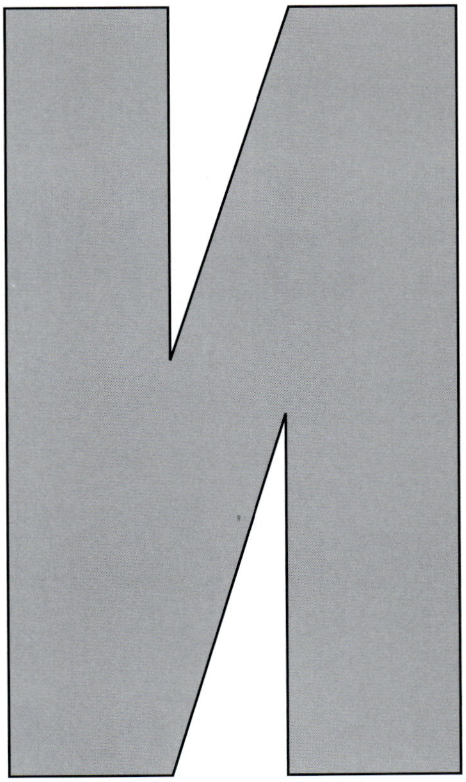

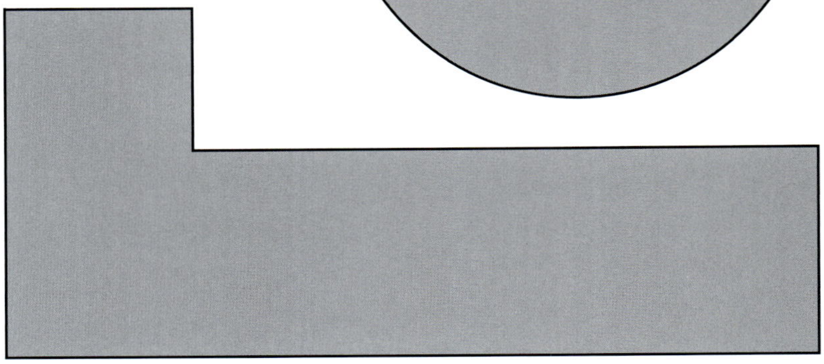

Pattern Templates

Lost Mitten or Glove Wreath

Lost Mitten or Glove Wreath

Can't throw away single mittens or gloves? Why not recycle them into this whimsical blue jean heart wreath! The lost hand warmers will remind you of days gone by.

Materials:

1	pair of light blue jeans
1	pair of dark blue jeans
1/2	yard print
1/2	yard fusible craft batting
2	packages extra wide double fold bias tape
8	mitten clips
7'	of stiff wire (I used twisted barbless wire)
1	mitten or glove

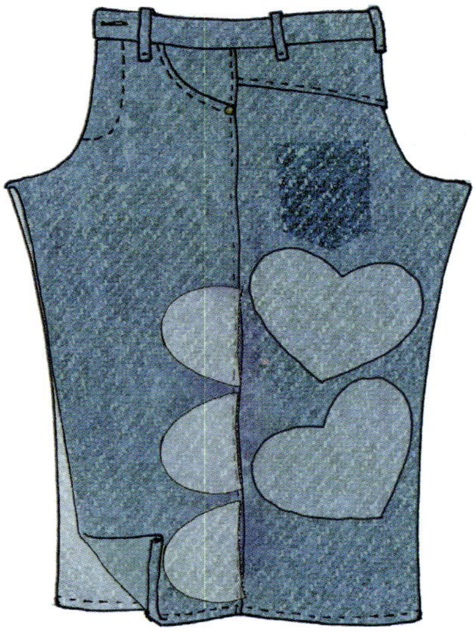

Cut:

1. Cut 2 full hearts from light blue jeans.
Cut 3 full hearts from dark blue jeans.
Cut 5 full hearts from print fabric.
Cut 5 full hearts from fusible craft batting.
Cut 4 heart halves from light blue jean (mirror image halves).
Cut 6 heart halves from dark blue jeans (mirror image halves).

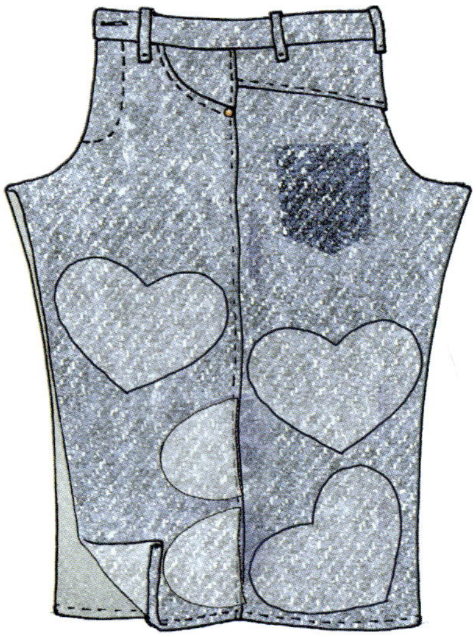

NOTE: Be sure to lay straight edge of heart halves along flat felled seam of jeans. That's the beauty of this project; there's no finishing to the half heart edge!

Lost Mitten or Glove Wreath continued

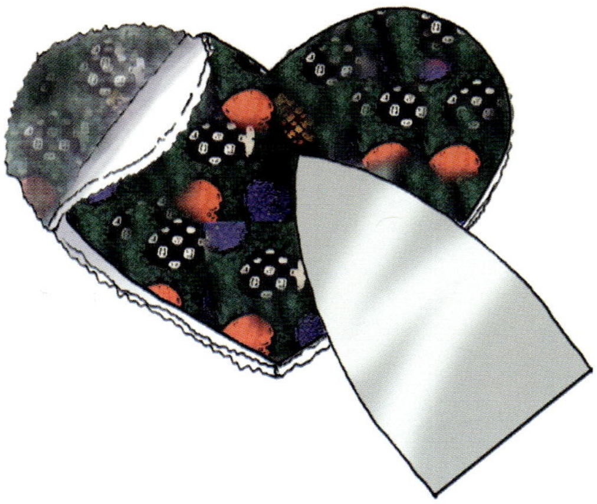

2. Layer full heart, batting and print as shown. Fuse together using wool setting and maximum steam. Pressing both sides may be necessary. Fusible batting adds needed body to the hearts.

Sew:

3. Use decorative stitch or zigzag to attach all 3 layers through the center.

4. Place heart halves on top of print keeping all raw edges together. Pin securely and stitch close to raw edge.

5. Starting at heart point, encase raw edges with double fold bias tape. Wider edge of tape should be on bottom. Pin securely. **HINT:** Pressing around curves will help shape bias tape.

6. Choose decorative stitch or wide zigzag and stitch around heart folding under bias tape and overlapping at starting point. Make 4 more hearts. Arrange hearts at curved edges and stitch together with bar tack or wide zigzag.

7. Connect lost mitten or glove in the center of hearts with mitten clips. Elastic on mitten clips may need adjusting.

8. Bend stiff wire into wreath shape approximately 80" in circumference. Twist wire together and tie bow to camouflage where wire joins.

9. Use 4 more mitten clips to attach wreath to wire frame.

These hearts could be tacked to a grapevine wreath or used to showcase a picture in the middle. Make single hearts and use as potholders. Instead of batting, recycle old towels, ironing board covers, and thermal underwear for potholder insulation.

Pattern Templates

Use this template for both Lost Mitten Wreath and Reversible Hearts.

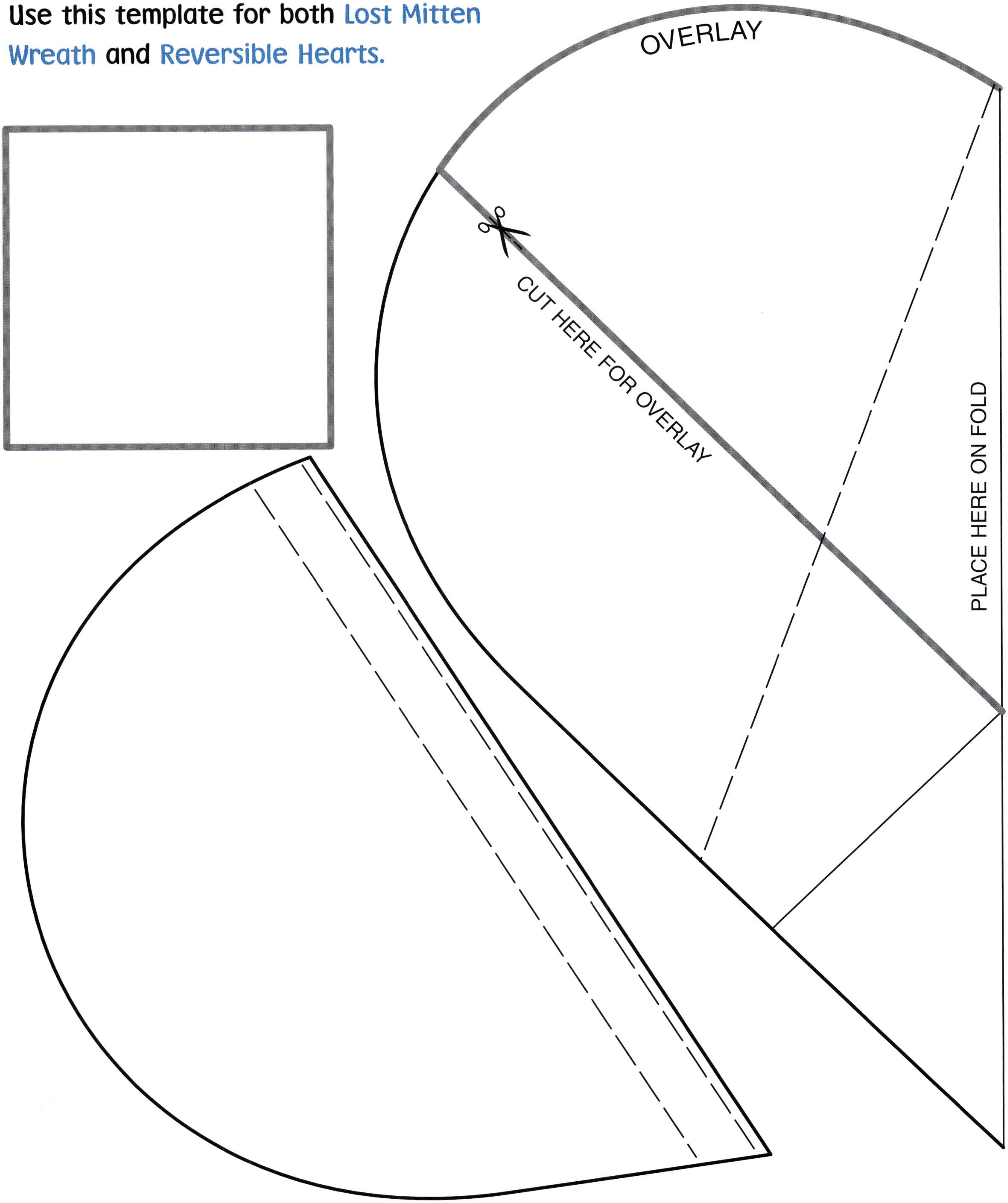

Reversible Hearts

Double duty describes this versatile heart wall hanging. One side can be themed for a holiday and the reverse can be used throughout the year for home décor. The previous chapter featured this heart design for the wreath and potholder. Old jeans take on a different dimension when attached at the points.

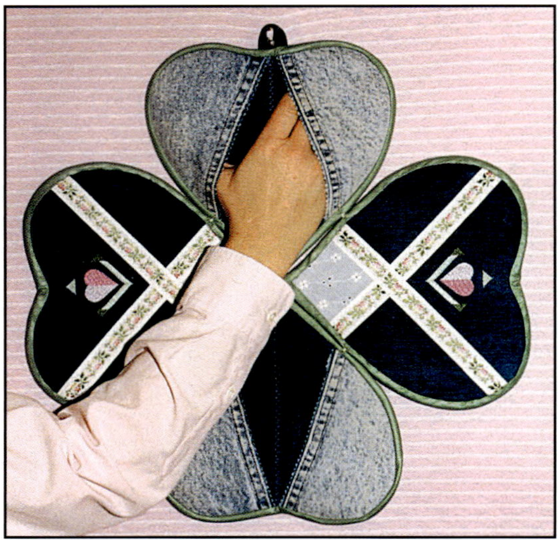

Reversible Hearts

Materials:

Horn of Plenty Hearts (side #1)

1 pair light blue adult jeans
1 yard sage green
1/4 yard Navajo print
1/2 yard fusible batting
1 1/2 yard embroidered ribbon 1/4 " wide
4 purchased appliqués (optional)

Embroidered Ribbon Hearts (side #2)

1 pair dark blue adult jeans
1 yard embroidered ribbon 3/4" wide
2 purchased appliqués (optional)
Scrap of white eyelet

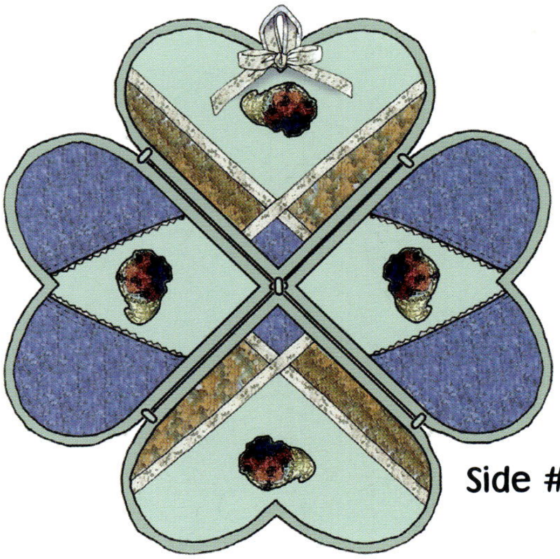

Prepare Side #1

HINT: If you choose to machine embroider holiday designs, do this on green fabric before cutting out hearts.

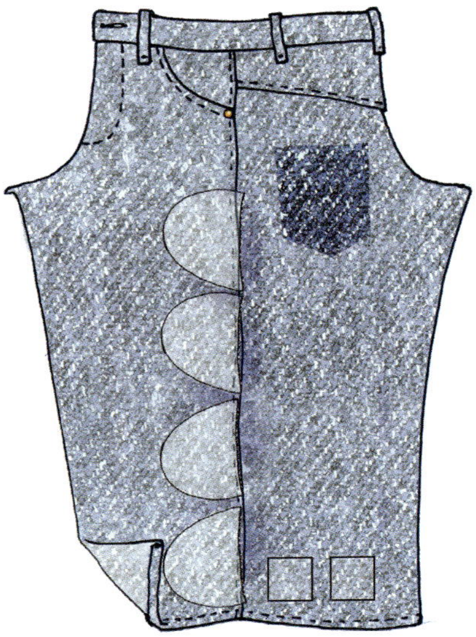

Cut:

1. Cut 2 sage green hearts.

Cut 2 Navajo hearts.

Cut 4 jean heart halves (mirror image).

Cut 2 jeans squares for heart point.

Cut 4 hearts from fusible batting.

Cut 2 sage green heart overlays.

Sew:

2. Stitch purchased appliqués to green hearts and heart overlays. The Janome Memory Craft 9000 and Memory Card #5 Holiday Series were used to embroider horn of plenty.

Reversible Hearts continued

3. Position green heart overlays and denim squares on top of Navajo hearts.

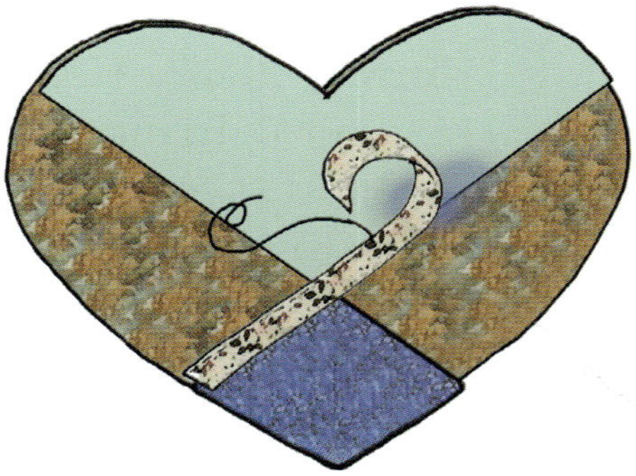

4. Cover raw edges of overlay and denim squares with embroidered ribbon. Topstitch both edges of ribbon. (I like to use a double needle).

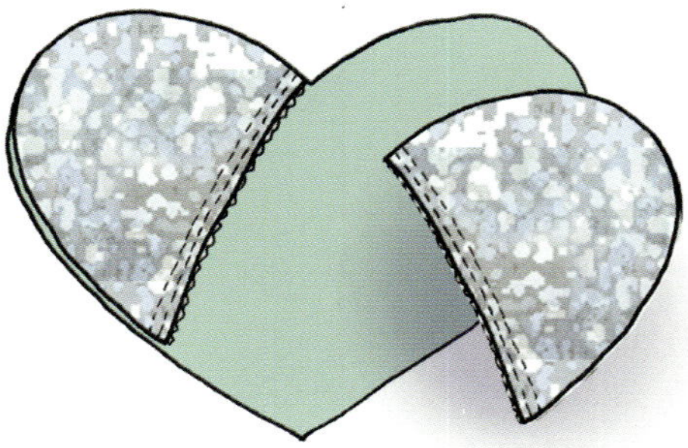

5. Place Jean heart halves on remaining green hearts. Lay aside.

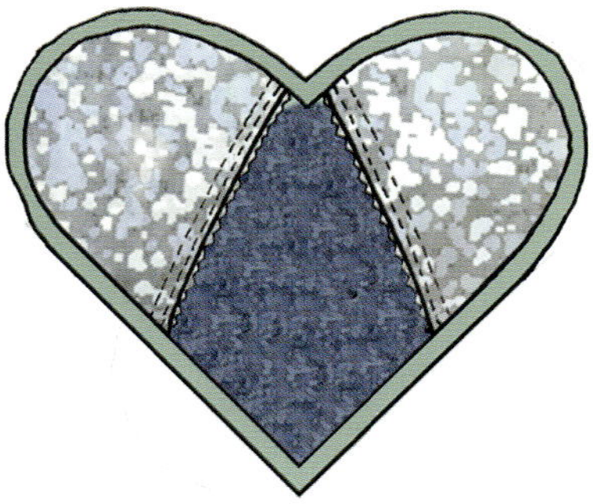

Prepare Side #2

HINT: Machine embroider jeans first and then cut out hearts centering embroidery.

Cut:

6. Cut 4 hearts from dark blue jeans.
Cut 4 heart halves from lighter blue jeans (mirror image).
Cut 2 eyelet squares.

Sew:

7. Stitch 2 purchased appliqués to jean hearts. The Janome Memory Craft 10000 and a design from the Small Floral Collection were used for this embroidery.

8. Position eyelet squares at points of embroidered hearts.

9. Cover raw edges of eyelet with embroidered ribbon extending the ribbon to curved edge of heart. Stitch both edges of ribbon.

10. Place contrasting heart halves on 2 hearts remaining.

11. Layer both sides of hearts with batting in center, making sure heart halves on each side are opposite each other. This reduces bulk when bias is applied.

12. Press fusible batting from both sides using maximum steam. (Fusible batting adds body to hearts. If using regular batting, press layers together with fusible web).

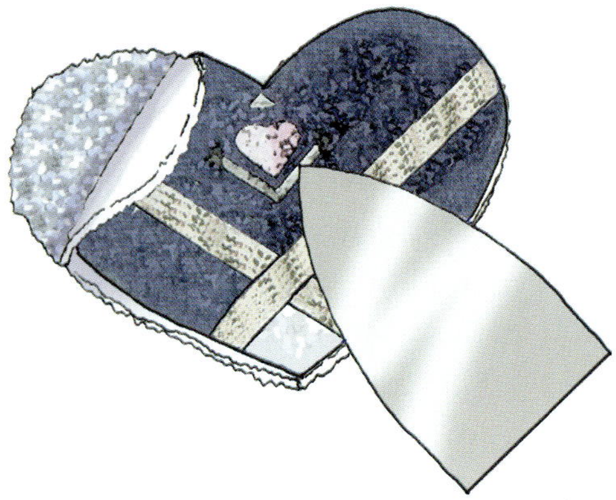

13. Pin all hearts securely and machine baste close to edge, through all layers.

14. Cut self- bias from sage green 1-1/2" wide and press **wrong** sides together.

15. Starting at point of heart, stitch raw edges of bias to raw edges of heart on either side. Roll folded edge of bias to opposite side and hand-stitch. This provides a neater finish rather than machine stitching because it is reversible. Follow this procedure on all four hearts.

16. To finish, bar tack all four points in center and tack heart edges about 4" up from center of all hearts.

17. Stitch ribbon over backside of belt loop.

18. Position belt loop on one side of hearts and stitch in bias ditch.

19. Attach ribbon bow to camouflage raw edge of belt loop.

This project is perfect for gift giving and the recipient will know that it came from the heart!

Resources

Bernina of America, Inc.
3500 Thayer Court
Aurora, IL 60504
Phone: 800-405-2739
Fax: 630-978-7609
www.berninausa.com

Brother International
100 Somerset Corporate Blvd.
Bridgewater, NJ 08807
Phone: 908-704-1700
Fax: 908-575-3721
www.brother.com

Clotilde, Inc.
B3000
Louisiana, MO 63353
Phone: 954-491-2889
Fax: 954-493-8950
www.clotilde.com

GET N' EVEN
Dancing Wheat
Respectable Love Story
P.O. Box 55
Clark, SD 57225
Phone: 605-532-5625
Fax: 605-532-5465
www.getneven.com

Handi Quilter, Inc.
322 East 500 North
Centerville, UT 84014
Phone: 801-292-7988
Fax: 801-294-3011
www.HandiQuilter.com

Janome America, Inc.
10 Industrial Avenue
Mahwah, NJ 07430
Phone: 201-825-3200
Fax: 201-825-1488
www.janome.com

Junk Jeans People, The
RR #3 Box 105
Clark, SD 57225
Phone: 605-532-5625
Fax: 605-532-5465
luveta@itctel.com
www.junkjeanspeople.com

Kaye Wood, Inc.
P.O. Box 456
West Branch, MI 48661
Phone: 1-800-248-5293
Fax: 989-345-3049
www.kayewood.com

Measurematic, Inc.
Miracle Ironing
Board Cover
995 West K Street
Benicia, CA 94510
Phone: 707-745-1138
www.miracleironingcover.com

Nancy's Notions, Ltd.
333 Beichl Avenue
Beaver Dam, WI 53916
Phone: 920-887-0391
Fax: 920-356-6175
www.nancysnotion.com

Rowenta Inc.
196 Boston Avenue
Medford, MA 02155
Phone: 781-396-0600
Fax: 781-396-1313
www.rowentausa.com

Snap Source, The
P.O. Box 99733
Troy, MI 48099-9733
Phone: 1-800-725-4600
www.snapsource.com

Sulky of America
3113 Broadpoint Drive
Punta Gorda, FL 33983
Phone: 800-874-4115
Fax: 941-743-4634
www.sulky.com

Viking Sewing Machines
31000 Viking Parkway
Westlake, OH 44145
Phone: 440-808-6550
Fax: 440-847-0001
www.husqvarnaviking.com